A Year of Playing Catch is a gem like baseball itself—everyday, interesting, thoughtful, and funny. It is an inside the book home run.

—Robert Benson, author of two dozen books, including
The Game: One Man, Nine Innings, a Love Affair with Baseball

Playing catch with my dad when I was a kid is one of my earliest memories. Those backyard catch sessions were a big part of my falling in love with the game of baseball, because of how they helped me connect with my dad. This book does a great job telling how a simple game of catch can help you connect with a loved one, make a new friend, or simply have fun.

—Curtis Pride, eleven-year major league veteran;
manager, Louisville Slugger Warriors

The beautiful austerity and challenging complexity of a simple game of catch are gloriously captured in Ethan Bryan's book. Each throwing partner during the course of a single year has a story to tell, and Bryan lovingly captures the essences of baseball and human connection in these brief but powerful vignettes.

—Perry Barber, umpire, *Jeopardy!* champion, and musician

Ethan's whimsical, fun-loving journey, told beautifully in this book, combined with his take on life and relationships, is a breath of fresh air. It also took me on my own unexpected journey of self-reflection that inspired me to once again chase my dreams, to make room for play, and to prioritize listening to people with experiences much different from my own. Grab this book and grab your glove. You won't regret it.

—Nathan Rueckert, artist and founder, The Baseball Seams Co.

In a world where genuine conversation feels like a lost art, this book shows us that a single commonality like baseball can create just that—conversations that open the floodgates to the heart of the human experience. Through the simple acts of playing catch and telling stories, Bryan connects unlikely co-stars in a tale of playful revelation, taking readers along for the summer tour of a lifetime.

—Tara Wellman, sport reporter and baseball podcaster

It takes a special person to capture the beauty and romanticism in the game of baseball. Ethan Bryan delivers the perfect pitch with this book. The genuine love that Bryan shows throughout his story allows readers a peek into the lives of those who eat, sleep, and breathe baseball.

—CHELSEA BROOKE LADD, FOUNDER, DUGOUT DISH

This is a beautiful look at baseball and life. You'll love Ethan Bryan's exceptional storytelling.

—JASON ROMANO, AUTHOR, *THE UNIFORM OF LEADERSHIP*; HOST, *SPORTS SPECTRUM PODCAST*

"Wanna play catch?!" Ahh, music to my ears. Reading this book took me back through a childhood of asking that question and especially the disappointment and the excitement of the answers. For the first time in decades, I thought about my childhood friend Billy, who always said yes. The disappointment when dad didn't have time to say yes was just as bitter when I read about Bryan and his dad. In Bryan's description of that new glove, I smiled at the memory of buying my first glove. Bryan's love and appreciation for baseball comes through on every page, but the real gift to readers is how he allows us to use his journey to retrace our own. What a gift!

—DR. KAT D. WILLIAMS, PRESIDENT, INTERNATIONAL WOMEN'S BASEBALL CENTER; AUTHOR, *ISABEL "LEFTY" ALVAREZ: THE IMPROBABLE LIFE OF A CUBAN AMERICAN BASEBALL STAR*

Much has been made in literary circles about the many good books that tell about the boys of summer and the smell of the grass and the crack of the bat. But nobody has told a story like this, a story of hope and whimsy and joy and the determination to play catch. To grab a glove, to have a catch, to hear that simple pop-pop-pop and enter some extraordinary space of true fellowship. Ethan Bryan is a wonderful writer, a clear storyteller, and he weaves in more fascinating sports history than you could imagine as he narrates this year-long memoir showing the redemptive power of play. This is a remarkable book for sports fans or anyone who has longed to explore her own field of dreams.

—BYRON BORGER, HEARTS AND MINDS BOOKSTORE

A YEAR OF

Playing Catch

A YEAR OF Playing Catch

WHAT A SIMPLE DAILY EXPERIMENT TAUGHT ME ABOUT LIFE

Ethan D. Bryan

ZONDERVAN BOOKS

ZONDERVAN BOOKS

A Year of Playing Catch
Copyright © 2020 by Ethan D. Bryan

Requests for information should be addressed to:
Zondervan, *3900 Sparks Dr. SE, Grand Rapids, Michigan 49546*

Zondervan titles may be purchased in bulk for educational, business, fundraising, or sales promotional use. For information, please email SpecialMarkets@Zondervan.com.

ISBN 978-0-310-36034-6 (audio)

Library of Congress Cataloging-in-Publication Data

Names: Bryan, Ethan D., 1974– author.
    Title: A year of playing catch : what a simple daily experiment taught me about life / Ethan D. Bryan.
    Description: Grand Rapids : Zondervan, 2020. | Includes bibliographical references. | Summary: "The tedium of daily stress leads us to play less and connect less than we long for—and our souls pay for it. Prolific author Ethan Bryan shares stories from a one-year experiment of playing catch every day and the inspiring lessons he learned about the sacredness of play, finding connections, and being fully present to the human experience"— Provided by publisher.
    Identifiers: LCCN 2020021853 (print) | LCCN 2020021854 (ebook) | ISBN 9780310360308 (trade paperback) | ISBN 9780310360315 (ebook)
    Subjects: LCSH: Baseball—Psychological aspects. | Baseball—Social aspects—United States. | Play—Psychological aspects.
    Classification: LCC GV867.6 .B79 2020 (print) | LCC GV867.6 (ebook) | DDC 796.35701—dc23
    LC record available at https://lccn.loc.gov/2020021853
    LC ebook record available at https://lccn.loc.gov/2020021854

Published in association with the literary agency of Mark Oestreicher.

Cover design: Curt Diepenhorst
Cover photography: sirtravelalot / Shutterstock; Aaron Foster / GettyImages
Author photo: Inner Images Photography
Interior design: Phoebe Wetherbee

Printed in the United States of America

20 21 22 23 24   /LSC/   10 9 8 7 6 5 4 3 2 1

To everyone who when asked, "Wanna play catch?" responded, "Yes!"

Contents

Preface

To ring in the New Year of 2018, I played catch with my younger daughter, Sophie. Thirty throws followed by a selfie. We used her phone to take a selfie, because it's hard to take selfies on my flip phone. I posted the picture on a seldom-used blog. It felt like a tangible way to honor the beginning of a year.

Later that same day, I played catch with my older daughter, Kaylea. We stepped out into our back yard, and the dog zoomed around us, doing everything she could to steal the baseball. We took a selfie as soon as we stepped inside, and I posted for the second time in one day.

And that is how Catch 365 was born.[1]

Every single day for an entire year, I played catch. The whole idea came about because of that singular day of catch with Sophie and Kaylea. They encouraged and challenged me to try it to see what would happen. I didn't know then that it would become one of the best years of my life. I didn't know then that dreams would come true. I could not have imagined all of the places I would go and all of the remarkable people I would meet as catch partners—more than five

---

1 Aaron Unthank came up with "#Catch365" for me to use on Twitter and Facebook posts. He messaged it to me late one night. I fell in love with the hashtagged moniker immediately.

hundred people in one year's time. As a former MLB player told me, "That's just a ridiculous number." Maybe that's because playing catch every day for an entire year is a ridiculous idea.

Thankfully, God seems to have a place for whimsy in this wonderful world.

Also, every single day for an entire year, I wrote an entry on my blog. I process life best by writing. The daily blog posts were for me, to make me laugh. I crack myself up. I also wrote the posts so I wouldn't forget that day's catch-playing story. I didn't keep track of 2018 by the actual calendar date. I kept track by how many days I had played catch. My mom thoroughly appreciated the daily updates.

Author Robert Benson is my writing mentor. The first time we met, we talked for hours over an incredible Italian dinner. At that dinner, he told me, "This world is desperate for good sentences, for good stories, and for those who are willing to do the hard work necessary to bring them to life."

Around day #70, Benson called and left me a message about that day's catch-playing blog post. "You are writing a book, my friend."

I have written books. The thought that I was writing a book about playing catch had not crossed my mind. I was thoroughly, constantly, forever preoccupied with trying to find future catch partners. Sending emails and messages via social media was a nightly routine. I was also somewhat worried that my elbow-shoulder-UCL-triceps-biceps might snap on the next throw and bring the quixotic quest to a screeching halt.

When it came time to actually write the book, Benson encouraged me not to write a diary. Once the year of playing catch concluded, over the course of three weeks, I wrote forty thousand words about the people I met and lessons I learned. I sent the first draft to a couple of my friends to read.

"I fell asleep in chapter two," one said.

"Not your best work," said the other.

I am blessed to have honest friends.

I consoled myself with a Dr Pepper, then deleted all forty thousand of the words and started over.

There are roughly three movements to *A Year of Playing Catch*. The movements are not equal in length. As much as that fact might bother some musicians, it doesn't bother me at all.

In 2018, my family took two, ten-day catch-playing road trips. The first movement follows the first road trip—the Catch 365 Tour of Hope, sponsored by the Baseball Seams Company. Throughout each chapter, there are stories of other catch-playing days which are notated with that day's number in parentheses. For example, I played catch with Emily (day #299) on her wedding day. I know it makes the reading a little bumpy; hopefully it will help keep the story straight.

The second movement shares the stories of therapy games of catch, finding a connection between tossing a ball and honoring the life and death of someone loved.

The third movement describes the final two days of Catch 365. The adventure finished in Kansas City just in case the Royals wanted to join in the fun during MLB's off-season.

There is a lengthy appendix in which I try to summarize the story of each day's game of catch in just a couple of sentences. I have double- and triple-checked and am praying I spelled everyone's name correctly. If I didn't, let me know and I'll send you an autographed baseball. Much like Pete Rose's, "Sorry, I bet on baseball," I'll sign, "Sorry, I don't know how to spell." I tried not to make it sound like reading a diary.

But before we load up the Bryan Family *Millennium Falcon* and travel throughout the Midwest, I want to jump ahead a few months, to a story in mid-July. Bob and Stan invited me to meet them for catch at the *Field of Dreams* movie site in Dyersville, Iowa. I convinced Dad to go with me.

I had no idea what to expect.

Baseball . . . can give us back ourselves. Baseball, if we love it, gives us back our place in the crowd. It restores us. Baseball, like life, throbs with hope, or it wouldn't exist.

—ANNE LAMOTT, *BIRD BY BIRD*

1

Keep Dreaming

TERENCE MANN: "There's something out there for me, Ray. And what a story it'll make: a man being able to touch the perfect dream."
RAY KINSELLA: "Then you'll write about it?"
MANN: "You bet I will."

—*FIELD OF DREAMS*

IT TOOK US TWENTY-NINE YEARS TO MAKE IT TO IOWA. TWO DAYS before arriving there, Dad and I left our homes in Springfield, Missouri, on a road trip. We have taken only a handful of such trips in our lives.

The summer after my senior year in high school, the same summer *Jurassic Park* released, Dad and I went to Myrtle Beach, South Carolina, for a short golf vacation. A couple of months prior, we were playing in a golf tournament together when the miracle occurred. Thanks to an almost perfect four-iron shot on an uphill, two-hundred-yard par three, I won a closest-to-the-pin contest and received two airline tickets to anywhere in the continental US. We redeemed the tickets and spent three days playing golf on some of the most amazing courses I've ever seen, complete with alligators in the pond and my first trip to the ocean. We fed the pond alligators leftover biscuits from breakfast in exchange for lucky bounces on the golf course. It seemed to work. And then I went to college and got married and left for seminary and got a dog and had kids, and Dad and I had to wait twenty years for our next trip.

Dad and I spent the summer of 2014 playing cowboy, traveling to small towns competing in Single Action Shooting Society contests. Competing under the alias Fret Maverick, I participated in timed shooting contests using guns reminiscent of the Old West, learning how to properly handle a rifle, shotgun, and pistol. For the first time, I heard Dad's stories of growing up in Colorado and his still unrealized dream of being a villain in a western movie.

That same year, in August 2014, Sungwoo Lee, a superfan of the Kansas City Royals from Seoul, South Korea, traveled to Kansas City to cheer on his beloved baseball team in person. Sungwoo learned English watching baseball games on the American Forces Network. The first time he saw on TV fireworks exploding over the fountains in Royals Stadium, he fell in love with both the stadium and the team. Two years before he came to Kansas City, Sungwoo and I became friends via Twitter, where we looked for whatever silver linings we could find as we watched the Royals invent new ways to lose baseball games. (The Royals were quite creative during those seasons, too.) Sungwoo had been saving up for years and finally made a trip to his field of dreams, traveling to the States to visit Royals Stadium (now known as Kauffman Stadium). The Royals promptly responded to his presence by winning seven consecutive games. When the Royals extended an invitation for Sungwoo to throw out a first pitch, Sungwoo invited me to be his catcher. He said it was a gift for my fortieth birthday and a thank-you for trying to provide a positive perspective. Dad and I made a day trip to

Kansas City so I could play catch with Sungwoo. That night, we celebrated as the Royals moved into first place with a win over the Oakland A's.

That year, the Royals made it into the postseason for the first time in twenty-nine years. Sungwoo came back to Kansas City from Seoul to watch the Royals in the World Series. His epic story is now featured in an ESPN *30 for 30* short documentary titled *#BringBackSungWoo*. I won playoff tickets to watch the Royals' American League Championship Series sweep of the Baltimore Orioles, and Dad accompanied me. That was our last trip together.

Until Iowa.

The classic baseball movie *Field of Dreams* released in 1989, the summer before my freshman year in high school. I saw it with my parents and connected with the tale of mysterious voices and ridiculous dreams. It has long since been one of my favorite movies. In the final scene, farmer-turned-baseball-field-architect Ray Kinsella, played by Kevin Costner, gets one last chance to "have a catch" with his dad, portrayed by Dwier Brown. Just reading the words from that scene softens my heart, stirring dreams of simpler times and days long gone. Here's the scene as written in the final draft of the screenplay:[1]

RAY (KEVIN COSTNER): You catch a good game.

JOHN (DWIER BROWN): Thank you. It's so beautiful here. It's like—well for me, it's like a dream come true.

Ray cannot speak. He nods.

JOHN: Can I ask you something?

Again, Ray nods.

---

1   Internet Movie Script Database, https://www.imsdb.com/scripts/Field-of-Dreams.html, accessed January 2020.

JOHN: Is this heaven?

Ray smiles and shakes his head no.

RAY: It's Iowa.
JOHN: Iowa. I could've sworn this was heaven.

Ray stops and looks intently at John. He asks this question as if he were asking the secret of life. Maybe he is.

RAY: Is there a heaven?

John takes time to answer that. He looks up at the night sky and searches it.

JOHN: Oh, yeah . . .

Then he looks square into Ray's eyes.

JOHN: Heaven's where dreams come true.

Ray looks toward the house and sees his wife and daughter on the veranda, a moon bright as butter silvering the night above them. He smiles. He finally understands. He turns back to John and nods.

RAY: Then maybe this is heaven.

John smiles wisely in return.

JOHN: Well . . . good night, Ray.
RAY: Good night.

John starts to walk off toward the door in the outfield fence.

RAY: Hey!

John turns back. Ray is holding a ball.

RAY: You wanna have a catch?

John closes his eyes for a second, and when he opens them, there is the hint of moisture. Does he know Ray is his son?

JOHN: I'd like that.

Ray tosses him the ball, picks up a glove lying there, and puts it on.

They throw the ball back and forth.

Dyersville, Iowa, is northwest of Chicago, almost where the Mississippi River separates Iowa and Wisconsin. Dyersville is a neighboring town of Middle of Nowhere. It has a population of around 4,200, roughly twice the number of students in my high school. Even though I'd wanted to visit the field for decades, Dad and I didn't make the trip on our own initiative. We went because Stan emailed Bob and Bob invited me.

On Thursday, January 11, Stan Sipka sent the following message to Bob Dyer.

> Hi Bob,
>
> I'm one of the millions who read and enjoy your column in the Beacon. I've seen on Facebook there is a guy who wants to play catch with someone every day. I would like to schedule a day, but I don't know how to contact him. I would be one of the oldest individuals to throw to him and we both would enjoy the time. I played last year and my record was 0–1. I'll bet you get a lot of crazy emails!
>
> Stan Sipka

Bob Dyer is a veteran columnist for the *Akron Beacon Journal* of Akron, Ohio. He tracked down my blog and sent me an introduction to Stan, an eighty-three-year-old man who takes his gloves on vacation with him. "I'm known as the guy who walks the beach at Hilton Head and asks old guys if they want to play catch," Stan said. "I always ask their wives if it's okay. One lady asked her husband where he had his life insurance policy in case she needed it. Most of the wives just laugh and comment that they will not massage sore muscles later."

When Bob emailed and suggested that he, Stan, and I meet at the Field of Dreams, I responded with a resounding, "Yes!" even if my heart wasn't convinced. It was only three weeks into the new year, and my arm and soul already were exhausted.

I ended 2017 and began 2018 in the middle of some kind of midlife crisis. A "freelance writer," I had a book project nearing completion and was excited to have a new one to start on, but neither book would bring in much money. Two months later, the new book was canceled. I wrestled with the answers to questions an English teacher named Mr. Nichols once asked me at the start of my sophomore year in high school: "Who are you and where are you going?" According to my growing stack of bills, I desperately needed gainful employment. But even more than dollars and cents, I needed a fresh breath into my soul. I wanted a calling I could call my own and pour my life into.

I chose a New Year's resolution: "Play golf with Dad at least once every month." I don't make decisions like that lightly. I make decisions like that intending to chase after them with all of my heart. Like the year I wrote about going to Royals games and watching Alex Gordon transition into a top-notch left fielder. Or the year I wrote a new song every month. I thought 2018 might be the year I got back into playing golf by making regular trips to the driving range and putting greens, entering a few tournaments, and attempting to get my daughters interested and involved in the sport. Maybe 2018 would be the year I would finally make my first hole in one.

My youngest daughter, Sophie, is an artist. Her ability to see something and then recreate it with watercolors or acrylics or just pencils truly astonishes me. I struggle drawing stick figures. Like most artists, she is sometimes unaware of the messes she leaves in her creative wake.

About a week before Christmas 2017, while she was still in school, I decided to surprise her by picking up her room. My intentions were honest and noble. I wasn't snooping. I just happened to see a plastic sack in the corner and figured it to be trash. But when I picked it up, I saw a brand-new baseball inside. Immediately I knew it was part of my Christmas gift. I returned the sack to the corner, picked up the laundry surrounding it, and put it out of my mind. I never said anything to Sophie.

On Christmas morning, I opened Sophie's gift. On the baseball, carefully handwritten, were the words, "Dad, Wanna play catch?" I was honored by the *Field of Dreams* reference and interpreted the baseball as a gift certificate. With this baseball, I could ask Sophie to play catch with me at any time and she would gladly and joyfully agree. (I later learned this interpretation was incorrect.)

On New Year's Day, a little stir-crazy and battling the post-holiday blues, I asked Sophie if she wanted to play catch.

"Outside?"

"Yeah, outside."

"At a baseball field?"

"Sure. At a baseball field."

"Okay."

The wind chill on New Year's Day morning was 1 degree. We layered up and drove to Fassnight Park, a seldom-used softball field near Parkview High School in Springfield, Missouri. Covered stone bleachers behind a chain-link backstop used to seat a few thousand spectators for semiprofessional fastpitch softball leagues. The sun was quite bright and no snow was on the ground. There was no one in the bleachers; there was no one else in sight. We did a few quick stretches, shoulders and triceps and back and legs, and started with underhand tosses. Each exhalation was a puff of smoke. I tried to put my favorite baseball glove on over the leather gloves I was wearing, but my hand wouldn't fit, so I took them off and threw them on the ground. My bare fingers felt the full effect of the freezing temperatures, even inside my Wilson glove. Every couple of throws, my fingers stiffened more. And every couple of throws, I took a few steps back until I reached a distance of around forty feet. We each threw the ball thirty times, an arbitrary number really, but one that was inspired by Cleveland Indians general manager Mike Chernoff in a story he told me for *America at the Seams.*[2] My eyes were watering, my teeth were chattering, my nose was dripping, and my fingers were stinging. Sophie was all smiles.

We took a quick selfie on Sophie's phone to document the adventure and ran to the van, where I turned the heat on high to get the blood flowing back into our extremities. "Keep your important parts warm," I remember Mom telling me when I was in college trying to survive wicked winter weather. I don't really know why I did it, but I posted the picture on a blog I occasionally used for poetry and random baseball writings.

Day #1
Fassnight Park Field.
30 throws.
1 degree wind chill.
Frozen cheeks, warm smiles.

After lunch, Kaylea called out to me from her bedroom while I was folding laundry and not paying any attention to whatever sporting event was on TV. Kaylea is my older daughter, a long-haired, curly-headed violinist who loves a good pun.

---

2 Published in 2017, *America at the Seams* is a book I wrote in partnership with Nathan Rueckert of Baseball Seams Company. It tells fifty baseball stories, one featuring and representing each state. Chernoff's story represents Ohio. Every month, he and his dad meet for a game of catch. Over the years, they've developed rules about what makes a game official. More information about the book can be found at http://www.americaattheseams .com/.

"I'll play catch with you."

We stepped out in the back yard and, avoiding the piles of frozen dog poop and the trampoline, each made twenty-five throws. As soon as we walked back into the house, our glasses fogged over. We took a selfie on her phone, and I posted for the second time that day on the same blog.

Day #1—Part 2

Back yard.

25 throws.

5 degree wind chill.

Tried to get a picture of the fogged-over glasses.

And then Inspiration whispered.

Why not play catch every day for an entire year?

The question captured my imagination and I couldn't focus on anything else. Ten-year-old me was delighted with the idea and ready to get started. Forty-three-year-old me was convinced the effort would end in some kind of surgery. I have multiple cool scars from major surgeries. I have no desire to add to my collection.

I feared such a project would interfere with "real life" and tried to imagine what worst-case scenarios might look like—holidays and vacations, and what if someone I know dies? Would I play catch at the graveside? Who can predict all the twists and turns a year might hold? I'm an optimist. Imagining worst-case scenarios has become a standard decision-making practice for me. If I can live through the worst-case scenario, I'm willing to take a chance to see what stories unfold.

Much like the story of farmer Ray Kinsella building a baseball field in the middle of his cash crop, no one ever said moments of inspiration have to make sense.

In *Together Is Better*, Simon Sinek writes, "A vision is like a dream—it will disappear unless we do something with it. Do something big or do something small. But stop wondering and go on an adventure."[3]

When Bob sent the email in January suggesting we meet in Dyersville in late July, I honestly didn't think my arm would make it. Throwing a baseball uses muscles that aren't used in the daily life of a writer. I was sore for weeks. I used enough IcyHot to once be accused of having some kind of menthol cologne.

But I was also having a blast. There was something freeing and joyful in getting away from the screen to meet someone and play, even in the middle of winter, even while wearing three shirts, a hoodie, long underwear, and two pairs of socks.

So toward the end of July, Dad and I made a trip to the Field of Dreams, the site of the movie, to play catch. We left on Monday and drove three hours to Kansas City, where I played catch with Royals broadcaster Joel Goldberg (day #204) in front of the Buck O'Neil mural. Every day, Joel spends time with my current Major League Baseball heroes, players with whom I can only dream about playing catch, players whose names are on the backs of my favorite T-shirts. As Joel and I played catch on the replica field just around the corner from the Negro Leagues Baseball Museum, he told me, "Much more important than any interview, answer, or question is building trust and relationships with these superstars, who are just human beings, who are just like you and me. When you build that rapport over time, when you spend time focusing on that relationship, the interviews become better, they become real conversations. It's all about relationships."

That night, Dad and I went to the Royals game and watched the team lose in heartbreak fashion to the Detroit Tigers, 5–4. We crashed

---

3   Simon Sinek, *Together Is Better: A Little Book of Inspiration* (New York: Penguin Random House, 2016), 16.

at a friend's place; Dad got the bed and I got the couch. We woke up the next morning to head to Dyersville.

Sunday, the day before Dad and I left on the trip, my Tuesday morning catch-partner canceled. I had less than forty-eight hours to find a new partner. This happened *all the time*. Tenacious adaptability is a must in any endurance effort. I emailed Nate Bukaty at the last minute in the hope he'd be available and willing to play catch.

Nate Bukaty is a sports talk radio host, the rare kind who isn't bitter or cynical. He was another person who spent time on the field of Kauffman Stadium befriending some of my favorite baseball players on the planet. When I lived in Kansas City, I enjoyed listening to Nate on the radio because he was a positive, hopeful voice and told great stories. Even during those seasons when the Royals played horrible baseball, Nate did a good job of putting the team and game in perspective.

"If I can work it out with my schedule, I'd be happy to join you for a game of catch," Nate replied. After several emails back and forth to coordinate, Nate invited me to meet him at the radio station.

On the way out of town, Dad and I stopped so I could play catch on day #205. Nate and I tossed a ball in the shade of the trees, standing on a strip of grass next to the parking lot.

"You don't go into this job for fame or money," Nate said. "It's all about the people and the importance of relationships. That's true for all of life, not just on the job. And never burn any bridges. No matter how much you might feel slighted or wronged, never burn any bridges. In fact, when you've been treated unfairly, do the opposite. The positive comes back around. That's true for all of life, too."

As Nelson Mandela said, "Sport has the power to change the world. It has the power to inspire. It has the power to unite people in a way that little else does. It speaks to youth in a language they understand. Sport can create hope where once there was only despair. It is more powerful than government in breaking down racial barriers. It laughs in the face of all types of discrimination."[4]

I wore a T-shirt while playing catch with Nate—Long Ball City's Pine Tar T-shirt—commemorating the infamous Pine Tar Game between the Royals and the Yankees. Thirty-five years ago to the day, Dad and I were watching when the Royals' George Brett homered off of Goose Gossage at Yankee Stadium, and then everything turned to chaos when Brett was accused of putting pine tar too far up the bat handle for a supposed advantage. Filip Bondy's book about the Pine Tar Game lives up to its subtitle: "The Kansas City Royals, the New York Yankees, and Baseball's Most Absurd and Entertaining Controversy." After I played catch with Nate, Dad and I stopped on the north side of Kansas City for gas and nourishment and watched on TV as *Air Force One* landed at the airport. President Trump was greeted by George Brett there. Combining baseball and politics is almost as dangerous as knocking on doors and talking to strangers about Jesus.

It was a six-hour drive to Dyersville from Kansas City. Dad and I listened to a James Patterson book on CD and took turns driving through the hills of northern Missouri and the plains and cornfields of Iowa. We stopped and ate a Maid-Rite burger for lunch because one of my catch partners, Officer Boomgaarden (day #54), told me I needed to try one. The book was great; I read the sequel when I got home. Lunch was great; I looked up recipes for how to make a Maid-Rite. The trip was uneventful, which Dad says are the best kind of trips.

After a fantastic dinner at a diner near our hotel, I had trouble falling asleep. I tossed and turned like a kid on Christmas Eve. I was too excited. My dreams were about to come true. I was going to see

---

4 "Celebrating the Legacy of Our Patron on Mandela Day," *Laureus*, July 18, 2019, https://www.laureus.com/news/celebrating-the-legacy-of-a-hero-on-mandela-day, accessed May 5, 2020.

the cornstalk-lined outfield and the white two-story house behind the wooden bleachers and climb on top of the mound and play catch.

I was forty-three years old when we finally made it to the Field of Dreams, five years older than the character Kevin Costner portrayed in the movie. After coffee and a complimentary breakfast, Dad and I left the hotel a little after 9:00, two hours before we were supposed to meet Bob and Stan. Under a clear blue sky, on catch-playing day #206, we drove through the cornfields and up the long gravel drive to the ballfield in the middle of nowhere.

I stepped out of the van and was amazed by what I didn't hear. No planes or trains or automobiles. Just the whistling of the wind interrupted by the pop-pop-pop of red-seamed baseballs hitting leather and so much genuine laughter.

As I filled a backpack with gloves and my camera and my computer and started walking toward the field, a pickup baseball game started on the infield. With the cornstalks behind me lined up like skinny outfielders waiting for a ball and a flag blowing gently in right field, Dad and I played catch. Pop-pop-pop. Smiles and laughter.

A lady walking her dog along the cornstalks stopped to take pictures and approached us. "Are you father and son?" she asked. "You are just the cutest things ever! I couldn't help but take pictures."

We played catch in center field, and it was a glimpse of heaven on earth. I wasn't worried about tomorrow or the trip home or trying to find people to play catch with me the following week. I was fully engaged in the moment, being with Dad and having fun living. Playing catch is easier than trying to find all the words to express our relationship. We took hundreds of pictures of the field and a selfie by the cornstalks. It was a reminder of all that was good from years past—strangers were connecting face to face through baseball. Baseball brought people together.

Dad and I were sitting on the bleachers watching the game on the field when Stan walked up. A handshake and a quick introduction and sixty seconds later we were tossing a ball. Pop-pop-pop. Smiles and stories and laughter.

Stan is a lifelong fan of the Cleveland Indians and has incredible stories of playing competitive baseball from high school through the Roy Hobbs League.[5] At fourteen, he threw a no-hitter in the championship game. At seventy-eight, he pitched against seventeen-year-olds and retired the side in order. He gave me lessons in how he holds his off-speed pitch.

"I am so appreciative that my wife let me do this," he said, "that she's supported me through all of the baseball stuff."

Looking back on more than two hundred consecutive days of playing catch, I agreed. My wife, Jamie, has been incredibly supportive and encouraging of this "mission . . . quest . . . thing." She sacrificed her camera for me to use for selfies because I was still using my old flip phone. She was saint-like as we talked through daily schedules and figured out who was taking which child where in what vehicle so I could coordinate with a catch partner. And she read the stories day by day and at least pretended to be interested for the sake of my ego.

When the mound cleared, eighty-three-year-old Stan walked up to the rubber as I knelt behind home plate. He flipped his glove and signaled his pitches and threw strike after strike after strike.

"This is really a great feeling, being out here on the field, throwing the ball. And I didn't fall off the mound. At my age, sometimes the feet don't go the way I want them to go."

After Stan threw a good session, Bob walked up and introduced himself. We shook hands and laughed. An email sent in the middle of January turned into a reality in late July. I commented on the Cleveland Indians' Omar Vizquel T-shirt he was wearing.

---

5   A competitive baseball league for adult players over thirty, named after the fictional protagonist from Bernard Malamud's book *The Natural*. In my opinion, this is one of those rare instances when the movie is better than the book.

"I wrote his autobiography with him," Bob said. "We played catch one day in my back yard. Highlight of my sports career!"

Bob asked about my arm and the adventure of getting to Iowa. It was good to finally talk and play catch with someone in person after several months of emails.

Bob took the mound and threw to me, then he threw to Stan, then Stan pitched to Bob and I took throws covering second base.

Bob then asked if I'd be willing to stretch out my arm in the outfield. We threw pop-ups and delighted in the blue sky and low humidity. Jack, a nine-year-old from Milwaukee, shadowed me. He reminded me of me. I asked him questions about his favorite players and teams. When I learned that he'd forgotten his glove, I teased him a little, then tossed him mine while I went to grab a different one. His parents came out to join us and I lent his dad my second glove so he and Jack could play catch, all the while keeping my eye on the infield in case one of the hitters sent one our direction.

In a little over three hours, I got in a week's worth of throws, though the only part of my body that hurt was my cheeks: I couldn't stop smiling.

I did not see Kevin Costner or James Earl Jones or Dwier Brown. I didn't see any ghosts or hear any voices. But I did play catch and made new friends, and Dad and I left the field with memories for a lifetime.[6] I sat in the passenger's seat and wrote the blog story for the day. After it posted, I sent a link to Dwier Brown, thinking he might like the father-son aspect of the story.

Though Dwier Brown appeared in the movie for only six minutes, his game of catch has become timeless, part of baseball

---

6   Just like in the movie, Dad and I connected with Moonlight Graham on the drive home. Tim Flattery (day #207) is the host for *The Moonlight Graham Show,* a podcast honoring underdogs and benchwarmers. We played catch in his back yard and recorded a podcast episode together.

and American culture. I found his contact information online, unsure whether he would actually read my message. He replied promptly.

> Ethan,
>
> Great writing. Congratulations on your continued success! Go the distance . . . (It would be a lot easier to have a catch year round here in Southern California.) I wish you all the best in your continued journey to 365! It is a noble pursuit.
>
> Your friend in the corn,
>
> Dwier Brown, aka John Kinsella

A couple of weeks later, Dwier was in Cleveland, Ohio, making an appearance at the Tristar National Sports Collectors Convention. Stan and Bob were able to connect with him for a game of catch. Bob wrote about it and sent me the link.[7]

The sign leaving the Field of Dreams says "Keep dreaming."

I have dreamed baseball dreams since I attended my first professional baseball game at the age of four. At that game with my parents at Royals Stadium, George Brett hit a walk-off home run in the sixteenth inning, and, much like Sungwoo, I fell in love with the stadium and the team. I didn't necessarily dream of fame or fortune. I just wanted to play baseball wearing the blue of the Royals.

After seeing *Field of Dreams*, I dreamed of visiting the movie site, placing it on a mental bucket list of eventually and someday. And because of a simple idea spurred by a game of catch with my daughters, I made it to the field and now dream new baseball dreams.

Maybe, like Stan, I can play catch and make new friends for the rest of my life.

---

7 Bob Dyer, "More Magic from the Field of Dreams," *Akron Beacon Journal,* August 18, 2018, https://www.ohio.com/akron/news/bob-dyer-more-magic-from-the-field-of -dreams, accessed January 16, 2019.

Like Bob, maybe I can write baseball stories with and about my favorite players.

Maybe Dad and I can take some more catch-playing road trips. Have gloves, will travel.

And maybe, someday, the Royals will have use for a catch-playing baseball dreamer.

Some dreams just take three decades to come true.

2
Growing Younger

Innovators are the ones whose dreams are clearer
than the reality that tells them they're crazy.
—SIMON SINEK, *TOGETHER IS BETTER*

I REMEMBER WELL THE ONE YEAR, THE ONLY YEAR, KAYLEA PLAYED
fastpitch softball. She was in fourth grade, used her mother's solid-black
Rawlings mitt, and was the league leader in getting hit by pitches. I
don't think a game passed all season without her getting plunked. Each
time the yellow ball struck her, whether in the leg or back or shoulder,
she took it like a champ, massaging the sore spot as she trotted toward
first base. Even the time the ball ricocheted off of her blue helmet, she
shook it off and promptly stole second on the next pitch.

Kaylea's sole season as a softball player was the same year I signed
my first contract as a writer, the same year I started writing my first
book, the same year I realized that working on staff at a church wasn't
good for my emotional health. That was the same year my family
lived in the basement of Jake and Jen's house while we tried to sell
our house. (Kaylea was a sophomore in high school when our house

finally sold.) We took a risk experimenting with communal living and learned about loving our neighbor through dishwashing, crying babies, and sharing sicknesses. Now whenever we visit Kansas City, we have a place to stay that feels like home. We took advantage of that relationship and stayed at Jake and Jen's house frequently during the catch-playing year.

At the beginning of her sole softball season, fourth-grade Kaylea participated in a free clinic for those playing baseball and softball in the Greenwood Sports Association. Former Kansas City Royals out-fielder Les Norman was the instructor. I thought the clinic would be a fantastic opportunity for Kaylea to grow her skills and was ecstatic that it was free. We pulled up to the fields only to discover that out of the sixty or seventy participants, she and one of her teammates were the only two girls. Kaylea felt awkward and nervous. She cast multiple looks in my direction which I understood as silent pleas to go home.

After everyone registered, before the clinic started, Les gathered the players around him in the outfield grass for introductory remarks. He said the skills they were going to practice that morning would be applicable to everyone, whether they played softball or baseball. One of the boys sitting near him commented loudly, "Softball? Oh, come on, that's not very hard."

Without hesitation, Les spoke in defense of fastpitch softball. He explained that because of the distance between the mound and the plate, fastpitch softball is actually harder than baseball, a lesson amply demonstrated when slugger Albert Pujols took his three swings against Olympian Jennie Finch and promptly sat down. Les commented that the girls who play fastpitch are every bit the athletes as the boys who play baseball. He shared a story about the girl who used to play on his baseball team and forced him to change positions because she was a better infielder than he was. The boy was silent for the rest of the clinic. Kaylea looked at me, beaming with pride at Les's remarks. She now felt comfortable staying for the clinic.

⚾ ⚾ ⚾

From the beginning of my experiment, I was aware that if I success-fully played catch every day of 2018, I would be playing catch when Kaylea started her senior year of high school. Central High School class of 2019. It all happened so fast. She grew up beautiful while I worried about paying bills.

I remember being a high school senior, being burned out on studying and having no idea what I wanted to do with my life. I remember the tests and essays and applications I had to do by hand because email and computers weren't even an option. I was so worked up about future unknowns that I missed a majority of the miracles of everyday life.

It's been twenty-five years since I graduated high school, and I have learned a little bit. I don't own a smart phone because I don't want to stare at a screen instead of seeing the faces of my daughters and wife and parents and friends. I have tried my best to encour-age my daughters to use their passions and gifts to engage the world, preaching that music and art breathe life and hope and help us to feel and see. I have tried to exemplify values I believe are important: per-sistence and courage and taking risks and making new friends. I have hoped, through conversation and example, to live out and pass along the wisdom found in Proverbs 3:5–6: "Trust in the Lord with all your heart and lean not on your own understanding; in all your ways acknowledge him, and he will make your paths straight" (NIV 1984).

I had no idea playing catch every single day for a year would be the best teacher.

⚾ ⚾ ⚾

In Ozark, Missouri, on the same highway my family takes to Silver Dollar City, at the same exit we take to catch throwed rolls at Lambert's Cafe, is U.S. Baseball Park. It used to be the home of the Ozark

Mountain Ducks, but the stadium closed in 2004 and sat empty for more than a decade. Driving past old, run-down baseball fields where there used to be laughter and play-filled sounds, where the crowd rose as one to celebrate something never before seen, where baseball dreamers were created is a silent, melancholy reminder that one day, everyone plays their last game. Under new management, the park underwent massive renovations, including the installation of astroturf and an enormous LED scoreboard, and reopened in the summer of 2016. The stadium is now home to the Drury University baseball team, multiple summer wood-bat leagues, and T-ball and coach-pitch teams.

I was thrilled to learn the Beijing Shougang Eagles and the Aussie Spirit were coming to U.S. Baseball Park as part of a tour by the National Pro Fastpitch League, the only fastpitch softball league in the United States. I sent multiple emails in the hope of connecting with someone for a game of catch.

Throughout the year, social media helped me make connections to catch-playing friends across the country. It also opened me up to ridicule from strangers—"This guy has no friends and no life!"—and countless rejections and misunderstandings. I received one email reply stating, "I love helping kids out with school projects! What grade are you in?" I never answered. Thankfully, Cheri Kempf, commissioner of the NPF, replied to my request.

"This year, the NPF league will celebrate its fifteenth season. . . . The league rosters some of the world's very best players in the sport of softball, including former Olympians, NCAA champions, players of the year, and Women's College World Series MVPs," Cheri said in her email.

Now all I had to do was show up with a glove and throw a ball in front of professionals. It was late May and day #142 when the NPF came to Ozark. Even after five months of playing catch every single day, I still got nervous. Nervous that an elbow or a shoulder might pop and I'd be finished. Nervous that I was just going to make a complete fool of myself. Nervous enough I couldn't sit still until after our game was complete. There's a fine line between being nervous and being excited. It took hundreds of days, but I eventually learned to embrace the excited side of new adventures more than the nervous.

U.S. Baseball Park has blue seats, limited shade, and an impressive, eighteen-foot-tall outfield fence from foul pole to foul pole. I walked into the stadium shortly after the team from Beijing arrived. Coach Teresa Wilson was visiting with the ballpark owners, so I hung back until an appropriate time to introduce myself. With my backpack over my shoulder, I waited while my heart hammered. When all of her questions regarding the field and facilities were answered, Coach Wilson turned my way.

"You must be here to play catch," she said. "I have the perfect player for you to meet."

Her nickname is Little Bear. She wore #42, a number which always catches my attention, but not because it's the answer to the ultimate question of life and the universe. It is the number retired in all of professional American baseball to honor the courageous legacy of Jackie Robinson. Chai Yinan, at only seventeen years old, is the youngest player on the Beijing team, a team that is gearing up for the 2020 Olympics. With her hair shaved short under her white ballcap, Little Bear sported the team colors of red and white—white pants, red warmup jacket, and red tall socks. (All the cool players wear tall socks.) Little Bear was also taller than me by at least a couple of inches. But what really caught my eye was Little Bear's glove. A pure white Marucci mitt with a spiral web. I had never seen a spiral web. I was mesmerized by both the color of her glove and its design.

⚾ ⚾ ⚾

I love looking at baseball gloves, paying attention to the makes and models the pros use as well as those of my youngest catch partners.

From the six-fingered Rawlings Trap-Eze glove to the unique design of first baseman's and catcher's mitts, I think baseball gloves are works of art. Throughout the year, everywhere I went, I carried a backpack full of my old gloves in case someone needed one to borrow.

Dad bought his first baseball glove in 1970, the year he and Mom married. A Wilson A2601, twelve-inch, Matty Alou–signature pro model. He bought it to pitch in a church softball league and used a leather engraver to inscribe his last name along the outside of the thumb. That glove saved his face on a couple of different occasions, protecting it from sharp line drives hit right back up the middle. I used it whenever Sophie wanted to play catch.

Shortly after we moved to Springfield, the summer before I started second grade, Dad bought me my first glove. A Wilson A2275, ten-inch, Mike Flanagan autograph model. Dad taught me how to break it in, positioning the baseball in the pocket, tying it closed with shoelaces, soaking it in water, and hanging it out to dry. That was the glove I used when he taught me how to catch pop-ups on a hot, dusty summer afternoon at a Little League field that no longer exists. That was the glove my youngest catch partners preferred.

Dad bought me my last glove at the beginning of my sophomore year in high school. Standing in front of a wall of gloves at Bass Pro Shops, it took me hours to narrow down the selection and decide. I chose a Wilson A2124, twelve-inch, George Brett autograph model with a woven web. That reddish-brown glove accompanied me through my last season of competitive baseball and has traveled the country with me from coast to coast. I used it to play catch when I spent a semester at the University of South Carolina and when I went to seminary in Texas, on the beach in California and on the grounds of Disney World in Florida.

After Bob sent the invitation to meet at the Field of Dreams, I started looking for a vintage glove, a glove similar to the ones used by the ghost players in the movie. Of course, I would be using the glove

Dad bought me, too, but I thought an experience that was almost thirty years in the making deserved something special. I turned to social media for help and was pointed in the direction of Play OK Antiques. Brett Lowman is a library media specialist at an elementary school near Springfield, Massachusetts, who followed in his father's footsteps as a collector and now a dealer of antique gloves. I told him about the experiment and searched through his extensive online catalog. He replied with pictures of a mid-1940s Wilson with split fingers, and immediately I knew it was out of my price range.

"I grew up a fan of the Royals and George Brett," he said in his message. "In 1985, at my first game at Fenway Park, a Royals fan gave me a foul ball that Brett hit. Glad to help out a Royals fan who is doing something cool."

Brett donated the glove to the catch-playing cause.

Even though the padding was minimal, I loved it. I used it all the time, from day #34, when I played catch at the Negro Leagues Baseball Museum standing next to a bronze statue of Satchel Paige, to playing catch with Dad in Iowa. Walking up to a field with the old Wilson in hand became one of my favorite icebreakers. Catch partners wanted to try it out and see how it felt, how it worked. We marveled at the abilities of players from decades past who used these simple gloves to stop blistering line drives and catch mile-high pop-ups.

On day #82, I played catch with Luke Lohman, a lean, brown-haired eighth grader who looked me in the eye. We were throwing the ball hard to each other, stretching out our arms while I talked with his mother, when it finally happened. Leather laces that had endured twenty-eight years of being sunbaked and chewed on finally snapped. The fingers of the George Brett glove simply flopped when I tried to open and close the web. For the first time all year, I hadn't brought any of my other gloves as a backup. I caught the rest of Luke's throws on my palm because there was no pocket.

"Does that hurt?" his mom asked.

"Not too much," I lied.

When I got home, I took a picture of the broken glove and posted it on Twitter, tagging the Chicago-based glove-manufacturing company. Wilson replied.

"Hey, Ethan! We're really sorry to hear about the glove. It happens, unfortunately—gloves need to be relaced from time to time. We'd be happy to help if we can. We can relace it for you—our glove team is finishing up some spring-training visits, but they'll be back next week and can take care of it for you—or we'd be happy to send you a new model from a few that we have left from spring training. Let us know what you'd prefer!"

On Major League Baseball's opening day (day #88), at a catch-playing, poetry-reading, and storytelling day at an elementary school, I used my brand-new Wilson for the first time. A blond-leather, H-webbed, A2000 outfielder's mitt with red stitching on the logo. The leather was so stiff my left hand was sore for hours afterward. It took weeks to break in the new glove.

Jeff Newlin (day #52) owns the Play It Again Sports franchise in Springfield. He invited me for an indoor game of catch before the store opened one morning in February. The throwing lanes were quite narrow, squeezed between shelving and workout equipment, but he was used to it. He even hit me ground balls after we warmed up. Before I left, he donated a solid-black leather Wilson for southpaws should I befriend any left-handed throwers in need of a mitt.

These six gloves, these six Wilsons, back down to five by year's end, were my constant travel companions. I used them all regularly, sometimes even switching between them during a game. Almost always, there was a glove between the front seats of the Bryan Family *Millennium Falcon*. I'd reach down and put it on and pop a ball in the pocket while waiting at stoplights. I figured that was better than staring at a screen. If any catch partners needed to borrow a glove, unlike most professional ballplayers, I was delighted to let them take their pick.

I freely confess that I am unreasonably attached to my gloves. I still carry them in a backpack, and they are on my list of things to grab should our house ever catch fire. Gloves are a reflection of personality and a trophy serving as a reminder of games of catch in the street or great plays in the outfield. Wearing a glove sparks memories and dreams and simple delight.

$\oslash$ $\oslash$ $\oslash$

Little Bear's glove said that she knew her best days on the field were ahead of her. She was young and cool and an athlete in top shape. She was still learning about herself and how to be her best self as she played the game. My gloves said I was old and probably had loose strings on the verge of snapping in both my arms and legs. My gloves said my best days on the field were decades behind me.

"Little Bear loves people, she loves to play ball, and she is a terrific ambassador of the game," Coach Wilson said.

In the middle of flyover country, I was getting ready for a truly international experience, playing catch with someone who didn't speak any English. My Chinese education mainly consisted of Springfield's cashew chicken and a few words I picked up from a friend in high school. My nervousness was amplified because we were about to play catch with a softball, and a softball has never felt right in my hands.

Coach Wilson escorted me onto the field and toward the first-base dugout. Little Bear and an interpreter were introduced to me, and the three of us walked down the right-field line. I stood on the foul line and did light stretches as Little Bear backed up into shallow right field.

I could *hear* her first throw.

The ball sizzled through the air the way I imagine lightning sizzles through the atmosphere, and exploded into my mitt. I was extremely grateful to be wearing the new glove; every last bit of padding was a necessity. I continued stretching as I threw, trying to find the best way to grip the ball, softly returning throws as straight as possible.

The interpreter informed me that Little Bear is a pitcher, so I held up the ball to her and mimicked a knuckleball. She nodded and smiled and soon we were communicating perfectly through glove flips, much like any major-league or minor-league or high-school battery. Fastballs and curveballs and a few sliders. Of course, she didn't throw her hardest, which I appreciated. Little Bear even gave me a thumbs-up after a couple of my pitches.

I shook her hand and we posed for a few pictures, and I found a seat to watch Little Bear's team warm up. From the team introductions to the last out of the game, the Eagles were full of energy, shouting cheers and encouragement that echoed off the outfield walls. My general admission ticket afforded me the freedom to change seats as often as I desired, so I relocated almost every inning, enjoying the various perspectives.

The pitcher for the Beijing team still had a no-hitter when I made the connection that Little Bear and Kaylea were the same age. Immediately, I felt *old*. A few weeks after this game, Kaylea would be on her first international trip, visiting Germany and France and Switzerland on an educational tour. I wondered if Little Bear's parents were as nervous allowing her to play ball all over the world as I was letting Kaylea stretch her wings and experience other cultures. I wondered about Little Bear's ball-playing history, who encouraged her to keep at it when she was just starting out, who were her earliest heroes. I wondered if Little Bear would tell stories to her parents about playing catch with the old man while in the United States like Kaylea told me stories of the entertaining and engaging street musicians and artists in Europe. Hopefully, Little Bear saw my game of catch as an extension of midwestern hospitality, celebrating her skills and honoring her hard work as the youngest player on the team. The wordless conversation was filled with smiles and gestures. Coach Wilson was correct: Little Bear was a fantastic ambassador of the game.

Beijing pitcher Wang Lan was dominant. In the fourth inning, Australia finally got their first hit, but it mattered little. Lan pitched a complete game, allowing only one run on three hits. Beijing won 5–1.

⚾ ⚾ ⚾

Near the end of my catch-playing year, I met Justin Perkins (day #332). Justin has a hobby job of relacing gloves to help pay for some of his children's extracurricular activities. He took the George Brett glove and gave it the royal treatment: oil, replacement padding, and new, *blue* laces. He took the old, worn-through, and broken-down glove and gave it new life.

Old made new. An apt summary of the catch-playing year.

With every game of catch, loose strings of muscles and tendons were strengthened. If it was possible, with every game of catch, I was growing younger. Maybe my best days on the field are still in my future. As George Bernard Shaw said, "We don't stop playing because we grow old; we grow old because we stop playing." Or maybe Satchel Paige said it best: "Age is a question of mind over matter. If you don't mind, it doesn't matter."

3

The School of Catch

Education: that which reveals to the wise, and conceals
from the stupid, the vast limits of their knowledge.
—*MARK TWAIN*

AFTER LIVING IN GRAND JUNCTION, COLORADO, FOR ONE YEAR, JUST
thirty miles from the Utah border with views of the Book Cliffs mountain range at the end of the street, my family moved to Springfield,
Missouri. In the days of blue laws, Dad started his own business as a
veterinarian making house calls, and Mom stayed at home with me
and my sister. That fall, I enrolled in Delaware Elementary School as
a second-grade student.

When I was six years old, all of my hair fell out. Patches on my
pillow as I slept and in the bathtub when I bathed. Mom and I visited
several doctors, who continued to state the obvious: "Your hair is falling
out." My condition was diagnosed as alopecia areata, and to this day,
I wake up with perfect hair. But I was the only bald kid at Delaware.

I'm pretty sure the rule was "No hats in school." No one told me
directly, so I wore a navy baseball cap almost every day, including

picture day. The portable photo studio was set up on the back of the wood-floor stage. The goldenrod curtains were pulled closed with PE classes taking place on the other side. Thirty-four years later, I stood on the same stage in front of the curtain as part of a book launch, giving every student and teacher in the building a copy of my first picture book, *Superheroes Are for Real.*

Back in second grade, I sat down between the camera and the neutral background with my cap pulled down tight just over my eyes. The photographer asked if I'd like to take the cap off for my picture. Then when I started to take it off, he suggested I leave it on. He probably didn't have any makeup to apply to my super shiny head, although he did ask me to tip the bill up to reduce the shadow covering my face. That picture can be seen every Christmas on an ornament Grandmon created for me.

⚾ ⚾ ⚾

As a school, Delaware has a unique and beautiful calling. Out of the thirty-five elementary schools in Springfield, and probably because of its central location, Delaware is one of the few chosen to educate students with disabilities and special needs alongside typical students. When I finished my work in class and had extra time, sometimes I was allowed to volunteer in other classrooms. On multiple occasions, I "worked" with Sarah. Sometimes I read books to her, and sometimes we just played. From her specially designed wheelchair, Sarah smiled and gestured and used a computer to communicate with me. I had no idea how it worked and was fascinated because her computer made it possible for us to become friends.

At the end of second grade, I was invited to play on my first baseball team—a Chuck E. Cheese–sponsored, Kiwanis League team. On this team, everyone learned about the various positions and tried on all the equipment, which was the perfect recipe for a lice outbreak. When

Coach called Mom to tell her the news, she replied, "I knew there would come a day I would be thankful God made Ethan bald." Coach was embarrassed, but it was a sign I had been accepted as a ballplayer.

Wearing red pants and red stirrups and a white T-shirt with our first names over numbers on our backs, my team was the Redskins. The profile of a Native American chief was centered on the front panels of the hat. When I was eight years old, I thought nothing of it. I figured our team was so named because most of us went to Delaware Elementary School, home of the Indians, and as a tribute to the football team out of Washington. We wore red and white because *almost* everyone in Springfield was a fan of the St. Louis Cardinals. I didn't know then that the term *redskin* was a slur, a word born of hate and prejudice.

⚾ ⚾ ⚾

In late March 2018, catch-playing day #86, I was invited to tell stories to the new inductees of Kappa Delta Pi at Missouri State University, the International Honor Society in Education. Anytime I get an invitation to speak at my alma mater, I do everything I can to take it. My four years at Missouri State University, at that time named Southwest Missouri State University, were a period of personal growth and deep learning. It was while I was at MSU that I finally started to believe I could write, even though Mr. Nichols had encouraged me regularly throughout my high school years. It was while I was at MSU that I experienced real answers to personal prayers. It was while I was at MSU that I met Jamie, my wife. On a stormy and windy afternoon, I spoke to the students in exchange for a game of catch. Dr. Kayla Lewis, a professor of literacy and the sponsor of the society, tossed a ball with me in the front of a lecture hall before the event started.

I caught Kayla by surprise when I showed up to the formal event in my MSU baseball jersey, which had been given to me by baseball head coach Keith Guttin (day #31). I figured wearing a baseball jersey was a true representation of me and the stories I wanted to tell. Kayla caught me completely by surprise when she told me she is Chickasaw.

I do not know how best to describe the feeling when someone's story shakes your soul to its core. When they trust you enough to open up their hearts and their lives, it's a sacred moment. When the weight of their story creates a holy collision from which there is no going back, the only way I know how to respond is with a deep, respectful, full-of-awe quiet.

"It's part of who I am," she said. "I view everything through a different lens, seeing the need for diversity everywhere. I incorporate multiculturalism in all I do. As a literacy professor, I have the joy and responsibility of doing it through books."

The Chickasaw tribe was originally from Kentucky and the Mississippi Valley. They were relocated to Oklahoma via the Trail of Tears and now have their headquarters in Ada, Oklahoma. Only sixty thousand Chickasaw citizens remain, and of them no more than thirty are fluent speakers of their native language. Kayla stressed the importance and responsibility of passing the Chickasaw language on to the next generation.

"When the violent colonialists came in, they said, 'You are not worthy to be you. Who you are is not worthy to be alive.' They came and took our land, took our culture, took our children all the while believing it was divinely mandated. They said we were heathens, that we were living the wrong way. What if we went to Europe and tried the same thing? The white people wanted to strip us of everything and turn us into someone completely different. This language is a part of culture and history and we cannot allow it to be gone forever," she said.

Quiet.

For multiple throws, I didn't say anything. I *couldn't* say anything. My heart was pounding listening to and processing Kayla's story. When I finally spoke, I asked Kayla to teach me a few words of the Chickasaw language.

Chokmá means "hello." *Chokmashki* is "thank you." *Chipisalacho* means "see you soon."

Playing catch with Kayla was one of several occasions when I experienced a worldview-shaping collision between my comfortable experiences and my catch partners' stories.

Andrew Cline (day #289) is a media and journalism professor at MSU. He's also a documentarian working on the story of two doctors who are treating Syrian refugees and the discovery of human devastation syndrome.

"Millions of Syrian children are having their lives completely torn apart by war," Andy said. "This is the same generation that's going to have to rebuild Syria. So the documentary is about the mental-health crisis of Syrian children who survive this war. The only way I can think of preventing it from happening to other kids is to show the horror of it on the screen."

Quiet.

Adam Robles (day #157) is a perinatal software specialist whose family suffered through Hurricane Maria in Puerto Rico and lived without power for four months.

"Thankfully, my family is okay. I was just in Puerto Rico, and there's a lot of rebuilding taking place. It's still pretty overwhelming when I stop to think about it."

Quiet.

Before he was a history teacher at Kickapoo High School, Phil Hockensmith (day #361) was a Russian specialist for the army during the Cold War.

"The US spends far too much resources on defense," he said. "We can't keep spending more than sixty percent of the national budget on the military stationed around the globe. That is impossible to sustain. We must act together with other nations to solve problems we can't solve alone: Climate change. Drugs. Opioids. And our treatment of veterans is a national disgrace. Greed and avarice have taken over as guiding principles instead of national interest. Combining the corporate world with the political world has been the recipe for a self-serving government. We must take money out of politics. Politicians must be servants first and have the same benefits as the people. They need to work together. They need to set the example."

Quiet.

Raj Suresh (day #279) is a stand-up comic from India who taught me about immigration and cricket. After playing catch, Raj and I continued to stay in touch via social media. His struggles challenged me throughout the year.

"I followed all your rules," he wrote. "Spoke your language in your accent. Paid your fees and filed the papers. I stand in line to this day while Britishers and Australians can enter this country overnight and work most jobs they want. What makes one immigrant better than the other? Is it the color of our skin and the geographies we were born into? We didn't choose either one, but we are punished for both. Every immigrant should be treated with an equal chance of entry and acceptance, provided they want to make a place better. And until this broken, lopsided legal immigration system is fixed, illegal immigration will continue to exist. I love America, but every day I wonder more and more—What part of this is brave? What part of this is free?

"This week makes it Day 3,888 in America," he said. "I received another piece of approval paperwork that lets me stay on for three more years. Days until green card—roughly 2,190 more. I've lost count of the cost for filing fees, attorney, and so on. I've been here since I was seventeen. I signed up for this, so I'm not complaining. I'm just saying that if we think legal immigration is the path forward, we must also ask who this system is designed to keep out: this same timeline is generally only a third as long for almost all Europeans and Australians, if not shorter."

Quiet.

Playing catch was an education with the best curriculum: stories. It was not only physical exercise, it was a daily workout in empathy, communication, and compassion. Thanks to my catch partners, I received first-rate instruction in being a better human.

⚾ ⚾ ⚾

After living for a decade in Kansas City, Jamie, Kaylea, Sophie, and I moved back to Springfield and Sophie enrolled as a second-grade student at Delaware. Life had come full circle. A year later, Jamie went back to school and earned her master of special education degree. The classroom where I used to play with Sarah is now the classroom where Jamie teaches.

Jamie works with students who have multiple disabilities and engages them in learning at their level. A couple of times each school year, I visit her classroom with guitar in tow, singing for and with her students. "The Wheels on the Bus" is always a hit, as is "If You're Happy and You Know It." Each time I visit, I stop by Stephanie Young's office to give her a hard time. Principal at Delaware for five years, Stephanie is a passionate St. Louis Cardinals fan, and her office reflects her fandom.

When she's not principalling, Stephanie can often be found working for the Double-A Springfield Cardinals, a minor league affiliate of the St. Louis team. Being at the ballpark helps her get a unique perspective on the community. "I worked fifty games last season," she said. "My favorite part of the game is always the national anthem. I love when a good marching band plays. I also love when the preschoolers come in and sing. I even have a certain love for when it's not so good, because these people are singing for their country. I almost get teary-eyed when the entire stadium is silent. I love my country."

☉ ☉ ☉

Two weeks before the end of the school year, after obtaining proper permission, I met Jamie and her students at the Miracle League field (day #127).[1] Miracle League began in Georgia in the spring of 2000 with the purpose of "creating opportunities for children with disabilities to play baseball, regardless of their abilities."[2] The league has since spread across the country and around the world. Recognizing the difficulty of trying to field a ball or run the bases on uneven grass or dirt surfaces, Miracle League teams play on a custom, rubberized field which is suitable for wheelchairs, crutches, and other devices. Miracle League also uses a buddy system, partnering players with volunteers who insure their safety and help them to enjoy the experience of playing ball. On this occasion, I brought along gloves instead of a guitar. With all of my heart, I am convinced that playing catch is for everyone.

The leveled playing field made it possible for those in and out of wheelchairs to share space between the white lines. One of Jamie's students teased me because of my love for the Royals. One of her students cheered me for wearing an Alex Gordon T-shirt and a powder-blue hat. And one student laughed a full belly laugh every single time he threw the ball. Throw. Laugh. Catch. Laugh. Repeat. It was beautifully contagious.

While he was still a student at Missouri State University, Patrick Queensen (day #298) started Phelps Grove Outfitters, a T-shirt company celebrating life in Missouri. He designed a "Wanna Play Catch?

---

1   Learn more about this amazing organization at miracleleague.com.

2   From the website.

#Catch365" T-shirt to raise money for the local Miracle League in honor of Jamie's work and her students at Delaware.[3] I wore my shirt *all the time*.

⚾ ⚾ ⚾

Throughout all of my school years, I was obsessed with getting good grades. I was fortunate to have been born with a good memory and did not really learn how to study until college. I listened in class and skimmed textbooks and did the work necessary to get an A. But getting an A is not the same as getting an education.

The purpose of school is not to get high test scores or grade-point averages or class ranks, or to pit the scholastic achievements of US students against other nations' students, though that's what seems to matter to those who have lost touch with the daily life of students and teachers. The point of school is to create a hunger and a curiosity to learn about all aspects of life on this beautiful ball of dirt and beyond. It seems to me that students sit unengaged as they stare at screens because computers and technology have been introduced as the answer to trying to improve test scores. Access to computers does not guarantee getting an education.

During the school year, I watch Jamie come home with stacks of folders and papers, filling out paperwork on each of her students so they have the best chance at getting the help they need for a hopeful future. Each semester, more rules and paperwork are given to her, unrealistic and absurd expectations placed on her shoulders. It is easy to see how teachers burn out. They never stop working. Some school districts are now pushing for year-round school so students don't fall farther behind. Kids lose out on time to be bored and to play. Teachers lose out on time to breathe. The never-ending cycle of

---

3   See https://www.phelpsgroveoutfitters.com/store/p154/Wanna_Play_Catch%3F.html.

lesson plans and grading is made more burdensome by continuing education and new programming emphases and efforts to measure whatever it is state agencies want measured. Eventually, the passion to inspire the next generation is squelched by the latest innovation in teaching methodologies.

Or the horrible and necessary addition of live-shooter drills.

⚾ ⚾ ⚾

When the school year was finally over, I went to Delaware to help move furniture and clean out a mini refrigerator while Jamie prepped her classroom for the summer. Weeks earlier, Stephanie and I had agreed to play catch on a day when the Royals and Cardinals squared off against each other (day #143). The first day of no school was the perfect opportunity. She dressed ready to play, wearing red-and-white-striped Cardinals tall socks that perfectly matched her red-and-white-striped Cardinals tank top. She sported a bucket hat and brought along a bobblehead doll of her favorite player to cheer her on and serve as witness.

I am positive I played catch with fans of the St. Louis Cardinals more than fans of any other team. In Springfield, the home of the Springfield Cardinals, those who wear blue and cheer the KC team are definitely in the minority. Playing catch with Cardinals fans was never a jarring experience, but it was an ongoing education in humility.

On the front lawn of Delaware, where families had enjoyed an end-of-the-year picnic the day before, Stephanie and I relaxed and told stories of baseball seasons past. I asked question after question, listening and learning between the intermittent pop-pop-pops. Every single day, playing catch engaged and encouraged my curiosity.

"The best part of working at this school is the joy that exists among all of the educators," she said. "It doesn't matter what you teach, you will be affected by the special programming that takes place here. You have to believe in the mission, you have to believe in what is done all across this building, because you will be affected. Because we do believe in the mission, that results in people who are genuinely joyful educating the kids. These are our kids."

Quiet.

That attitude as a leader makes all the difference in turning a school into a place where lifelong education begins.

4

Baseball Brit and Simone
the Hall of Famer

Here is the world. Beautiful and terrible
things will happen. Don't be afraid.
—*Frederick Buechner*

In the summer of 2018, Springfield, Missouri, became an
international baseball hotspot.

Joey Mellows, a mustache-sporting, International Baccalaureate
economics and geography teacher from England, emptied his savings
and traveled the world to watch and write about baseball. He traveled
tens of thousands of miles, crossing timelines and continents, watching professional baseball at all levels, from the independent leagues all
the way to the majors.

"Have you ever wanted to roll the dice with your life and do
something completely different?" Joey questioned on his blog under
the moniker Baseball Brit. At the age of thirty, he learned he had a

non-life-threatening but chronic health condition. "I decided to seek adventure while my body was still capable."

Joey is doing everything he can to increase interest in baseball throughout the United Kingdom. He came to Springfield to attend his first Double-A game. The Cardinals hosted the Frisco RoughRiders. In general, Minor League Baseball does a fantastic job of engaging and entertaining fans. In specific, the emcees of the Springfield Cardinals are incredible. (I played catch with two of them, Jay Fotsch, day #128, and Jeff Houghton, day #164.) I knew Joey would enjoy the entertainment both on the field and between innings. Shortly after he got to town, I picked him up for a game of catch and to hear his global baseball stories (day #186).

"This is the first time I've played catch with a baseball. I used to play cricket, but you just use your hands in it. I don't own a mitt and have never thrown a baseball," he said.

Joey was a catch-playing rookie.

I loved playing catch with rookies and let them select a mitt out of my backpack, giving them a little information about each. I always encouraged them to use the new Wilson—the biggest glove, the most padding—though some were intrigued by the vintage glove. We'd start out close with underhand tosses and take steps back, gradually increasing the distance between us, doing everything possible to insure no one got injured. That was my singular, overriding fear for the entire year, that someone would get seriously hurt. It was why I avoided approaching major league players until the end of the season. I didn't think I could handle being that person who injured Alex Gordon or Whit Merrifield or Salvador Pérez in a game of catch. (As it turned out, when I did start asking pros, no one answered.)

Expect rejection; rejoice in exceptions.

Joey, however, wasn't a true rookie. His cricket experience easily translated to baseball. He used both the new Wilson and the old George

Brett model, getting a feel for the difference between outfielder's and infielder's mitts. By year's end, he'd even purchased his first glove.

"It's easy to get stuck in a rut," he said while fielding grounders and pop-ups. "Sometimes, you just have to take a chance and see what happens."

Joey and I both shared a passion for the great game of baseball. Because of that passion, we both found ways to connect with new people and to learn. Learn about baseball. Learn about the world. Learn about life. Some learning is hard to translate into words; it has to be experienced. Just like traveling the world to watch baseball was a risk for Joey, playing catch every day was a risk for me.

In good stories, there is always an element of risk. Ray Kinsella plowed down his crop to build a baseball field. Risk. Bilbo Baggins left the Shire in search of an adventure. Risk. Harry Potter walked alone and unarmed to meet Voldemort in the woods. Risk. Risk-taking is not just a one-time leap in the heat of the moment. Risk-taking is living out your deepest, truest convictions, whether or not the idea conceived in your imagination is ever born.

Thanks to a basketball game in East St. Louis on a mission trip, I have a repaired ACL, MCL, meniscus, and cartilage in my right knee. Thanks to a large, purple, plastic ball on a trampoline while I jumped and exercised with my daughters, I have a reconstructed left ankle, with two screws replacing the removed bone chip. I have no desire to spend any more time on the operating table or in physical therapy. At least once a week, the thought crossed my mind, "What if something pops? What if something tears?" Those questions born of worry and fear existed only late at night and between games. They vanished when I was playing catch. Such is the strategy of fear, whispering in the darkness to create doubt and raise anxiety.

Toward the end of the first chapter of her book *Big Magic,* Elizabeth Gilbert quotes poet Jack Gilbert. "We must risk delight. We must have the stubbornness to accept our gladness in the ruthless furnace of this world."[1] There is no journey, there is no learning, there is no gladness apart from risk.

Forty days after Joey visited Springfield, Taiki Hoshino (day #251) came to town from Isesaki, Japan. Taiki had been invited to perform judo demonstrations at the Japanese Fall Festival put on by the Springfield Sister Cities Association. He's also the catcher on his baseball team at Kokushikan University. Taiki is studying sports biomechanics, training, and conditioning. He loves the Saitama Seibu Lions of Japan's professional Pacific League, along with ballplayers Yu Darvish and Shohei Ohtani.

Taiki filled out a personal information form to better pair him with a host family during his stay. On the line asking for his interests and hobbies, he wrote, "Baseball!" My friend Merry Yeager, a massage therapist who helped keep my arm in good working condition and who was my catch partner on day #225, connected me to Taiki. At the same field where Joey and I tossed the ball, Taiki and I met for an early morning "catch-ball," as he called it.

When I was in junior high school, Dad decided it was time to buy himself a catcher's mitt—a Rawlings, Ted Simmons autograph model. The catcher's mitt was a sign of encouragement; I was finally throwing the ball hard enough that the padding in his old glove wasn't sufficient. Because of its size, however, during the year of playing catch, I did not regularly carry the catcher's mitt around in my baseball backpack. But when Merry informed me that Taiki was a catcher, I made certain to bring it along.

Taiki did choose Dad's catcher's mitt and offered to catch a bullpen session for me. I confirmed that the catcher's signs are the same in Japan as they are in the US: one finger for a fastball, two fingers for a curve, three for a changeup. I took my place atop the artificial mound, which was rotting plywood covered with green turf grass. I

---

1   Elizabeth Gilbert, *Big Magic: Creative Living beyond Fear* (New York: Penguin, 2015), 6.

toed the rubber and focused on his glove, then started really throwing the ball. Throwing with feeling. Throwing with intent. Throwing with heart. Each pitch was delivered with passion and a smile. Taiki framed each pitch as if waiting for the call from an imaginary umpire. Even in the steady rain, we were both having a blast. On multiple occasions, my plant foot slipped, because of a combination of the slick surface and the thoroughly worn-through tread on the bottom of my tennis shoes. My pitches sailed high or wide, but I didn't care. Neither did Taiki. I didn't want to stop, and Taiki kept pounding his mitt. Taiki complimented my pitches, nodding his head, pointing his glove, offering verbal commentary after each one.

"Fastball. Good spot. Nice off-speed. Good pitch." I understood his broken English commentary. I probably didn't break 60 mph, but it sure felt good to throw the ball hard.

"In baseball," Taiki said, "it is important to be a team player, to focus on teamwork. If I don't have friends, I can't play baseball."

All year long, I was keenly aware of the ridiculousness of carrying out a resolution that requires others to complete it. But the risk of playing catch every day was rewarded with the sheer delight of making so many new friends.

Baseball brings the world together.

⚾ ⚾ ⚾

On day #143, after playing catch with Stephanie the Principal, I went to U.S. Baseball Park for the second game of catch of the day, another opportunity to play with an international partner. I had connected with Fabian Barlow, the head coach of the Aussie Spirit, on the same day I played with Little Bear. We set up a game of catch for the following day. I assumed I would be partnered with another fastpitch softball player, so I left all my baseballs in the van.

Coach Barlow shook my hand as his players stretched out on the field. He then introduced me to Simone Wearne.

Simone was working as an assistant in a logistical capacity with the Aussie Spirit until she joined her team, the Australian Emeralds, as the manager in preparation for and competition at the 2018 Women's Baseball World Cup. Scheduled for late August, the tournament was being hosted in the US for the first time.

Simone is a trailblazer for women's baseball. She is one of the most highly decorated ballplayers period, with awards such as Tournament Co-MVP at the Women's Baseball World Series (2002), All-World Starting Pitcher (2006), Australian Baseball Federation Female Athlete of the Year (2008, 2009), and Women's Nationals Pitching Award Winner (2004, 2007, 2008). She was also Australia's team captain for the 2008 Women's Baseball World Cup in Japan.

"Simone is the first and only female in Australia's Baseball Hall of Fame. She's simply one of the best players in the world," Coach Barlow said.

There is only one female inducted into the National Baseball Hall of Fame in Cooperstown, New York. Surprisingly, it's not one of the players from the All-American Girls Professional Baseball League. The induction of a female into the Hall of Fame came about because of a special committee tasked in 2006 to evaluate Negro Leagues players who deserved to grace the hallowed space. For decades, Kansas City Monarchs legendary player and manager Buck O'Neil traveled the country championing the Negro Leagues and its players. He told stories of how Babe Ruth was a white Josh Gibson, how his dear friend Satchel Paige was one of the best pitchers ever, and how Oscar Charleston was Willie Mays before Willie Mays was Willie Mays. Because of the special committee, Effa Manley, the only female in the Hall of Fame, was inducted as an executive, not a player, along with seventeen other people associated with the Negro Leagues plus former MLB reliever Bruce Sutter. (Don't get me started on my Dan Quisenberry platform.)

Effa Manley was the co-owner of the Newark Eagles, the team that won the 1946 Negro Leagues World Series against Buck's Kansas City Monarchs. She had the passionate vision of a marketer and was an astute businesswoman. She used her position in the baseball world as a tireless advocate for civil rights, introducing Anti-Lynching Day at the ballpark. Manley died at the age of eighty-one, twenty-five years before her induction.

My first thought upon hearing Coach Barlow's introduction of Simone was simple: *I'm going to be playing catch with someone in the Hall of Fame.* Immediately, I regretted leaving the baseballs in the van. I didn't want to play catch with a Hall of Famer with a softball. I really didn't want to play catch with a *Hall of Fame pitcher* with softballs. But with skies rapidly darkening overhead, I decided it would be better to play catch and stay dry than to play with a baseball and get soaked.

Two things jumped out at me when I started visiting with Simone: her drink of choice and her glove.

"Dr Pepper is my favorite drink in the world," she exclaimed.

I agreed wholeheartedly and tipped my bottle of Dr Pepper in her direction.

Simone's glove was a sun-bleached blue leather with solid white paneling for the webbing. I didn't recognize the brand logo. Though most players have their names stitched into the leather, Simone's glove had two Chinese characters and her number just above the thumb.

"A friend gave it to me after knee surgery," she said. "It means 'warrior.'"

We stepped out onto the turf and walked behind home plate. I tipped my hat to Little Bear and Coach Wilson of the Beijing Eagles, then focused all of my attention on Simone. I did not want to be distracted playing catch with a Hall of Famer. I attempted throwing a knuckleball, but the softball was too big and too slick. For the rest of the year, I regretted not running back to the van to grab a baseball. Even though it started to sprinkle toward the end of our catch, I would have loved studying Simone's world-famous, Hall of Fame–worthy breaking pitches.

Two weeks after I met Simone, Ava and Carolina expressed interest in a game of catch. They are stepsisters living through the courageous adventure of a blended family. After we arranged a day to play catch, they posted the date on their family calendar. Carefully written were the words "A and C play catch," followed by a large smiley face (day #161).

"I think catch just seems like a lot of fun," Ava told me. Ava loves to read and wants to be a doctor.

"I've always wanted to give baseball a shot," Carolina said. Carolina is fascinated by dance and dreams of being a teacher.

I was playing catch with two more rookies who simply wanted to have fun. Playing catch is an exercise in growing a friendship, in establishing trust and cooperation. Playing catch is about enjoying that moment, in the shade, under the tree, and sharing life with those who are with us. Multiple times I stressed to Ava and Carolina that there was no need to apologize. We were all learning from each other. I shared a few stories about playing catch with Little Bear and with Simone, and listened to their stories of the adventures of stepsisterhood. I complimented both girls and gave them a baseball so they could keep practicing at home.

⚾ ⚾ ⚾

At the end of August, I was excited to watch the Women's Baseball World Cup. Of course, I wanted the US to perform well on their home soil, but I also wanted to watch Simone and see what I could learn from her managerial skills.

But the World Cup wasn't on broadcast television.

The most important event in women's baseball, a tournament that is played only every two years, a tournament featuring top baseball talent from around the world, could only be streamed online.

How are baseball rookies like Ava and Carolina supposed to learn that baseball is for girls too if they can't watch the best female baseball players in the world on TV?

Effa Manley was surely screaming from her grave at the outrageous decision not to air the tournament.

I have friends who boldly claim that no woman will ever be successful in professional baseball. I'm glad Mamie Johnson, Toni Stone, and Connie Morgan didn't listen to their detractors. These three women played in the Negro Leagues and proved they could stand toe-to-toe with players who were later inducted into the Hall of Fame. I'm thankful Justine Siegal didn't stop playing baseball because someone suggested that girls only play softball. She has since coached at the major league level and started her own organization, Baseball for All.[2] I'm thankful Simone Wearne played baseball, even if I didn't get the chance to watch her team on TV.

I would love the chance to be an ambassador of the game like Joey, sharing my passion and capturing the imagination of the next generation, inviting them to play and learn and have fun together. I'd be quick to share stories of my time on the field with Simone the Hall of Famer, as well as the stories of Effa Manley and other women who played ball. I hope that those who make business decisions for baseball will remember their days as catch-playing rookies, the joy they experienced when they first put on a glove and threw the ball, the wonder of staying up late to watch games on TV. I am convinced that baseball, playing catch in particular, is for all people. Creating space so everyone can play, from Australia and Japan to the UK and the US, is a minor risk that will create hope-filled ripples and new friends around the world.

---

2   See https://www.baseballforall.com/.

5
More Than a Game

You enter the extraordinary by way of the ordinary.
—*FREDERICK BUECHNER*

THE MISSOURI SPORTS HALL OF FAME HOSTED ITS 2018 SPORTS
Enthusiasts Baseball Luncheon at the University Plaza Hotel and
Convention Center near my home in Springfield. It was my first time
attending the event; I had no idea what to expect or how I should
dress. Eventually I settled on a polo shirt, though my heart would have
chosen a Royals jersey.

It took me a while to find a parking space, and the walk to the
convention center was far enough I started sweating. Two baseball
coaches held the doors for me and I headed straight for the bathroom
to towel off my head. One of the perks of being bald: you can go from
sweaty to squeaky clean in a matter of moments.

I timidly walked into the convention center space, which was
overflowing with baseball people. I spotted several catch-playing
friends, including former Pittsburgh Pirates Gold Glove and World

Series–winning outfielder Bill Virdon (day #61). I approached him at the head table and shook his hand.

"You here causing trouble?" he asked.

I nodded.

"You played catch yet today?"

I shook my head no.

"Shouldn't have any trouble finding someone in this crowd."

I already had a partner secured for after the induction ceremony, a friend and the brother of one of the inductees. Kim Bell also sat at the head table. She was present to accept Coach Bell's induction into the Missouri Sports Hall of Fame.

Coach Howard Bell was one of my first real baseball heroes. In second grade, I read George Brett's *Born to Hit* and Pete Rose's *Winning Baseball*. Both athletes had secured their positions in my personal hall of fame from an early age. But Coach Bell was a local baseball star, a real person from my hometown. Every morning while eating breakfast, I read the comics. After the comics, I read the sports page, and I remember reading about Coach Bell's baseball prowess, including his game-winning grand slam against the University of Missouri when he played for Missouri State. I think I'm one of the few people in Springfield who haven't yet seen the VHS of the hit.

I played baseball on the same team as Coach Bell's younger brother, Darrin. I am certain Coach Bell attended some of our games, but I never met him. After my family moved back to Springfield in 2012, one of the first headlines I read announced Coach Bell's ALS. My heart sank. I didn't want to believe the diagnosis.

When I was a student at Missouri State, I studied amyotrophic lateral sclerosis (ALS) as part of an honors biology class. I wrote a story about Lou Gehrig and his "luckiest man on the face of the earth" speech because the disease is commonly known by his name. I received a perfect score on the paper. After class, the professor asked if he could keep it. "It's the first time anyone's written a baseball story in my class. I loved it."

ALS attacks the muscular system while leaving the brain alone. Those with ALS waste away day by day, unable to get their bodies to cooperate with their brains. Not that diseases actually have intent, but if they did, ALS would be purely evil.

The year my family moved back to Springfield, Coach Bell and I became friends, talking about life and baseball and raising daughters. Mere weeks before he passed away of complications from ALS, I interviewed him. I had been working on a book, chasing baseball dreams, spending time with the baseball team from Drury University. The project took a turn in focus as our relationship continued to develop and is now published as *Striking Out ALS: A Hero's Tale*. Coach Bell's interview is part of the appendix of the book.

"What I have learned living with ALS is the importance of taking each day as it comes, being happy and enjoying the moments you have, because you never know what the next day will bring. Finding ways to live to the fullest every day is crucial, for each day in and of itself is truly a gift. The hardest part of life now is not being able to do the everyday things that everyone else seemingly takes for granted. Just like baseball, living with ALS is 90 percent mental and 10 percent physical. Taking this approach has made things easier in pushing through the daily struggles and obstacles."

Kim and Howard started dating in high school when she was only fifteen years old. They had dreamed of growing old together. After hearing the diagnosis, Kim wanted to be mad at God, asking, "Why Howard?"

"Howard set me straight every time with his simple comment, 'Why not me?' We believed God was using his situation for something positive, but it was so hard to find the good while watching Howard slowly become trapped inside a body that was no longer working," she said.

Springfield responded to the needs of the Bells and took care of them, allowing them the grace and freedom to truly focus on living and making the most of every day.

"Howard told me one time that most people die never knowing if their life mattered. He said he was so blessed because he was dying knowing that he had made a difference in the lives of so many people and he felt lucky. He wasn't afraid to die, but what I couldn't share with him was that I was afraid to live without him."

Coach Bell battled ALS with courage, grace, and humor. He passed away in 2013 at the age of forty-eight, just before MLB's opening day. We had talked about watching some of the games together.

Since his passing, Kim has become a dear friend. On the date of Coach Bell's fifty-fourth birthday, Kim invited me to play catch (day #103). She has started a new wedding venue on the north side of Springfield called The Barn at Belamour—*belamour* being both a French word meaning "one who is loved" and a creative combination of her last name and a word that sounds like the word for love.[1]

Even as she cared for his every need, Howard encouraged Kim to chase her own dreams.

"I've always been a party planner. It's just a part of me. About two or so years after Howard died, another wedding venue reached out to me, and that's what really sparked my interest to go ahead and start, to create my own space. On weekends, I'd drive around looking and dreaming, and I happened to see this land while checking out another location. This place was so overgrown, all you could see was the top of the barn. But it wasn't for sale, so I took some pictures and kept looking.

"Howard was always exploring, going new routes. He always drove home a different way from wherever he was. A couple of months had passed from the first time I had seen the property, and I know

---

1   See http://thebarnatbelamour.com/.

it sounds crazy, but I felt him pulling me down Farm Road 94. And there was a For Sale sign in the yard. I was the only person interested in the property. Everybody told me I was crazy. They were seriously worried about me. But after Howard's passing, Belamour gave me a new passion, a new purpose, and a new dream."

The Barn at Belamour is stunning. Fifty acres of rolling green and a house with a basement and two barns. The barn used for weddings was raised in 1891.

"I know it sounds cheesy, but I love the idea of people coming here to express their love to one another."

In the fall of 2018, Kim reached out to me and asked if I'd be willing to officiate a wedding at Belamour. I haven't performed many wedding ceremonies and always get nervous, worried I'll screw up the names or do something horribly wrong. But because it was Kim who asked and because the wedding was hosted at Belamour, I said yes.

On the day of the wedding, the grounds and barn and stage were breathtaking. It was an honor to be part of a couple's committing to love one another until death do them part. It reminded me of one of my favorite quotes from Yogi Berra: "Love is the most important thing in the world, but baseball is pretty good, too."

As Kim and I played catch, we talked about the different memorials to Howard around Springfield.

In the visiting section of the stands at Neil Pittman Field at Kickapoo High School sits a lone red chair. For a high school to honor the coach of a rival high school says something about both the character of the school and the character of the coach. Howard was a teacher at Glendale High School for almost thirty years. After his death, Glendale High named its softball and baseball complex after him and established a scholarship in his honor.

Kim laughed when I asked what she thought Howard would think of my playing catch every day.

"Howard had a chair he sat in in the garage, an old office chair.

Even when his ALS progressed, he'd sit in that chair and watch ball games. His nephew wanted to play catch—he was around three years old—so they rolled the ball on the garage floor to each other. Everyone in the neighborhood wanted to play with Howard. The doorbell would ring and they'd ask, 'Can your husband play?' If he could've played catch every day, he would have."

Forty-one days after Kim and I played catch, Coach Bell was inducted into the Missouri Sports Hall of Fame, along with pitcher Rick Ankiel and the historic St. Louis Browns.

"That caught me completely by surprise," Kim said, who accepted the honor on Howard's behalf.

"I just don't want to talk," Kim told me at the luncheon. "I'm not a speaker or a storyteller."

I affirmed she was the perfect person to accept Coach Bell's induction and left to find my seat as the ceremony started. I sat at a table of former Glendale players as the only representative from Kickapoo. By luck, I sat at the table next to Fred Buchholz, who was a former batboy for the St. Louis Browns. Fred was the batboy the historic day three-foot, seven-inch Eddie Gaedel walked to the plate as a pinch hitter wearing the number 1/8, one of owner Bill Veeck's brilliant promotional ideas for a cellar-dwelling baseball team. I've seen a tribute to Eddie at the National Baseball Hall of Fame in Cooperstown proclaiming him the shortest player ever to play the game. Baseball truly is for everyone.

When it came time for Kim to speak, she shared simple stories from the heart. When she finished, there were not many dry eyes in the room.

"Early in his career as a teacher and coach, Howard wanted to quit. Jack Stack encouraged him to give it one more year. Those words made all the difference. ALS is a death sentence. But Howard encouraged each of us to concentrate on living fully today."

After the lunch and ceremony, Darrin and Jake and I met for catch (day #144). Darrin is Howard's younger brother and Jake is Darrin's oldest son. The three of us traveled to the fields just a few blocks north of Jarrett Middle School, where Darrin and I were classmates in the late 1980s. We went to play catch as a celebration of life, Darrin in his St. Louis Cardinals T-shirt and I in my favorite Royals hat. We reminisced about our old team, the one named with a slur, and I immediately remembered one story.

I was the starting pitcher and Darrin was at shortstop. After a couple of innings, our team had opened up a pretty big lead, and Coach switched us. As I handed Darrin the ball, I heard the opposing coach shout out, "First the bald guy, now the big guy! Come on!" Darrin threw his warmup pitches and I hid my face in my glove and laughed.

Howard's exhortation to live fully each day was thoroughly reflected in my experiment, because playing catch happens in the present tense, when life occurs. A whole-body experience involving the coordination of hands, eyes, feet, brain, and heart, playing catch slows down the relentlessly steady beat of life's drum and focuses us on what is happening right now, each throw and catch a prayerful rhythm of connecting, of establishing a relationship, of enjoying this moment with someone else.

Trace the seams and find a grip.

Step and throw.

Wait.

Listen for the pop of the catch.

Wait.

Watch your partner throw.

Follow the ball all the way into your glove.

We are wise when we impart rhythms into our lives that help us focus on life in the present tense.

Darrin, Jake, and I spread out across the field, forming a catch-playing triangle. Out of sheer orneriness, I teased Jake and told him he needed to use the old Wilson glove, the one with minimal padding. After a couple of soft tosses, I asked if he wanted to keep using it. He politely declined. Sweat dripped from the bill of my powder-blue hat as Darrin and I remembered past seasons of baseball and basketball and the awkwardness of life in junior high. Like kids at recess, the three of us lived out scenes from *The Sandlot,* where play is the focus and no one is paying any attention to the passing of time.

Just as I had encouraged Kim, Darrin encouraged me. "I love what you're doing," he said. "There is beauty and power in its simplicity."

We are so good at complicating the joy of life. As we age, we need to seek out and create space for play in multiple forms as a reminder of life's beauty and simplicity.

Four months after the induction ceremony, Drury University and Missouri State University faced each other for the third time in The Battle for Bell, an exhibition baseball game honoring Coach Bell to raise money for the CoxHealth ALS Clinic. For the third time, I was unable to attend the game because of familial obligations.

Coach Bell's daughter, Kameron, agreed to meet at the baseball and softball complex at Glendale High School for catch the morning of the game (day #265). She played softball growing up and was the catcher for her team at Glendale. Bless her knees and ankles. I have the utmost respect for anyone who is brave enough to put on the gear and take charge of the game from behind the plate.

"Dad refused to coach me growing up because he wanted to just be my dad, not my coach. He spent so much of his life coaching other kids, and he wanted sports to be a different experience with me. When I was fourteen or fifteen, Dad and I would go out in the back yard and play catch. And he threw the ball hard, hard enough it stung my fingers every time I caught it. I'd get as far away as I could on the other side of the yard and he was still throwing the ball hard. When I was in high school, though, he did take the opportunity to coach me."

Whenever I hear stories of Coach Bell from friends in the community, they almost always center on how he treated others, how he listened to what they were saying, how important he made them feel.

"Dad was nice to everyone. It was just how he acted all the time. He stressed that we didn't know everything other people were going through and that being nice, being kind, is something we can always do. Making that extra effort to go out of your way and put a smile on someone's face can really make a big difference.

"At The Battle for Bell, I love remembering Dad, hearing stories about him and how he's still making a difference. Selfishly, I just love hearing his name. This exhibition game started because of him, and now it's so much bigger than just him. Some people come just to watch baseball or because they knew my dad. Some people come because they know someone with ALS. But everyone who comes really does have a good time, and they are supporting such a great cause."

Baseball is more than just a game. It is the celebration of relationship between parent and child, recalling days gone by and dreams for the future. It's more than wins and losses and all the statistics that sabermetricians analyze. It is a test of perseverance, passion, and heart, daring to dig in to the batter's box one more time, willing oneself not to give up in the face of enormous obstacles. It is not just entertainment or an escape from the stresses of daily life; it is the heartbeat of hope, where communities place aside differences and come together to cheer players of all nationalities, and especially those wearing tall socks.

And at The Battle for Bell, the game of baseball is giving back to the community, encouraging those living with a dreadful illness, teaching each of us to carpe our diems and believe that God can bring good from any situation.

6
The Living Art of Catch

I'm going on an adventure!
—*BILBO BAGGINS, THE HOBBIT*

I AM RELATIVELY ART ILLITERATE. I KNOW THE *MONA LISA* AND Monet's *Water Lilies* and Warhol's soup cans, though I'm not sure exactly why the soup cans are considered art. I know *A Sunday Afternoon on the Island of La Grande Jatte* as the pointillism picture featured in *Ferris Bueller's Day Off*, and *The Last Supper* in *The Da Vinci Code*. I know Michelangelo's *David* and the Sistine Chapel and Bob Ross, whose painting was once featured on a Daytona Tortugas jersey. But I've learned that art is so much more than famous pieces decorating museum walls and the occasional baseball jersey. Art is a form of communication, a wonderful way of opening up and expressing oneself through a created work. The whole point of art is to make a connection with someone, to make them feel something, and the first time I saw Brett Kesinger's art, I was floored. Brett taught me how to see art, how to experience and enjoy it.

For ten years, I was a youth minister in Lee's Summit, Missouri.

Brett was one of the cadre of faithful adult volunteers who helped me figure out what youth ministry in the twenty-first century looks like. One Sunday after church, he and his wife accompanied my family for lunch. Sitting at Jason's Deli and enjoying chocolate ice cream, Brett made a sketch with crayons on a napkin while we were talking about the Royals. That sketch is better than anything I've ever attempted to draw. A few weeks later, he came by my house and pulled up his collegiate portfolio on my computer. I was stunned. I savored his creations. I was in complete and utter awe of his designs. There were days I scrolled through his handiwork and just breathed. His art stirred hope in me.

Since that first lunch, Brett and I have partnered on several word and art projects of faith, hope, and ridiculous dreams. He created an eight-foot-wide nativity-journey painting on plywood, which is one of my favorites. He has designed covers for a few of my books, and his rendition of Kauffman Stadium with the likeness of Alex Gordon hitting is another favorite. I would love to have the walls of my house filled with his works.

It seems to me that creating art is an act of hope. In a world that is driven by the bottom line and uber-efficiency, art loudly challenges everyone not to take themselves so seriously. Art breathes into our broken world and extends an invitation to engage the present beauty. Art creates margin in the midst of the mundane, offering fresh perspectives and insight in exchange for an investment of time. My ridiculous hope is that somewhere in this world, there is a patron of the arts who sees Brett's work and pays him generously to create masterpiece after masterpiece.

⚾ ⚾ ⚾

On April 9, day #99 of Catch 365, as the year came to be known, Alamo Drafthouse Cinema hosted a special screening of *Field of*

Dreams. The event was advertised as a fundraiser for the local Miracle League in honor of Catch 365. I sent an email with the idea for the screening to Jennifer Johnmeyer, creative manager for the theater, who responded almost immediately.

"Ethan, I'm just gonna lay it out to you straight," Jennifer wrote.

That was all I could see before I opened the message. I wasn't sure I wanted to read the rest of her email. Most people who rejected my catch proposals didn't actually respond, and those who did certainly didn't do so with such bold words. I know I am capable of dreaming and scheming utterly absurd ideas and by no means expect everyone to immediately jump on board. Sometimes, though, I feel compelled to share my ideas just in case someone else catches a glimpse of the possibility.

I gathered the necessary courage and clicked.

Jennifer continued, "*Field of Dreams* is my favorite movie. My FAVORITE MOVIE OF ALL TIME."

I exhaled and read the rest of the message with a huge smile on my face. So I met Jennifer at Alamo, and we played catch the day of the screening and talked about her family's baseball museum in Nevada, Missouri. The James A. Novak Baseball Museum features the extensive personal baseball collection of Jennifer's grandfather.

"He was a baseball fan during a time when it was easier to connect with the players," she said. "He was pretty obsessed and started expanding his collection, going to games and trade shows all the time. And then he took up quilting as a hobby."

"Quilting?" I did not expect a baseball story to turn into a quilting story.

"He started making quilt blocks of players' names with their teams and stats. He'd make a quilt of an entire team, then send it off with a check asking if they'd autograph it. Most of the time, the teams would send back the check with all the squares signed. His collection filled up the attic and storage and his office space, so he bought a bank."

"Wait, wait. Again, sorry for the interruption. He bought a bank? Because of his autographed quilts?"

"Yes, he bought a bank, then filled the whole second floor of it with his baseball memorabilia. There's a Cubs room, a Red Sox room, a Kansas City Monarchs room, a room paying tribute to the stadiums that are no longer with us. His dream was to open it up with free admission, taking donations with all the proceeds supporting the local Little League, helping kids who couldn't afford to play the game. He got to see his dream come true, too, but passed away shortly after that. For the past year, my dad's been renovating the outside of the bank, restoring it to its original splendor, and now he's working on the inside. Hopefully, the museum will reopen soon."

From my very first email, Jennifer understood the heart of playing catch and the importance of Miracle League. She saw the great possibility of turning the idea into a reality. Thanks to her efforts, the proceeds from the screening covered the costs of fourteen players in the Miracle League.

⚾ ⚾ ⚾

At the screening, my family sat in the back row and sipped water while the story and stirring melodies unfolded before us. The idea solidified at the exact moment Ray Kinsella and Terence Mann set out from Boston to find Moonlight Graham in Chisholm, Minnesota. I know you're not supposed to talk during a movie, but I couldn't keep the idea to myself. I knew it was equal parts audacious and crazy. I leaned over to Jamie and whispered as quietly as possible, "We have to go on a road trip. A catch-playing road trip."

Shortly after I committed to playing catch every day of 2018, my story was featured on CBS, ABC New York, MLB.com, and *Inside Edition*. My inbox was filled with catch-playing invitations from coast to coast.

Corey in Atlanta.

Garrett in Virginia Beach.

Scott in Pennsylvania.

Shaun and Shane in Illinois.

Nicole in Huntsville.

Heather in Rhode Island.

Lisa and her three sons in Denver.

David in Pigeon Forge.

Nathan in Maryland.

Katie in New York.

Craig in Raleigh.

The Daytona Tortugas, a Class A-Advanced affiliate team for the Cincinnati Reds, invited me to come play catch at Jackie Robinson Ballpark, the first stadium where Jackie played as part of affiliated baseball. He wore number 9 for the Montreal Royals at that spring training game.

I also received invitations to the Netherlands and the Dominican Republic, but I didn't have a passport.

There is no possible way I could have imagined any of this when I played catch with Sophie and Kaylea on January 1. My intentions were simple—kick off a new year doing what I love most, playing catch and spending time with my daughters. I had no real reason for taking a picture and posting a couple of sentences on the blog other than the hope of creating a conversation about baseball in the middle of a cold winter. My wife was confounded by the attention.

"Why do so many people care about you playing catch?" she asked over dinner.

I laughed and shrugged.

Much to the disappointment of six-year-old me, I am not independently wealthy like Bruce Wayne and cannot afford to travel the country on a whim to play catch. But as soon as I whispered the idea to Jamie in the movie theater, it refused to leave me alone. When I committed to playing catch every day, I jumped in with both feet. I promised not to let my enthusiasm wane or just go through the motions with any of my partners. I gave the project all of my heart and trusted that something good and beautiful would come of it. The timing for planning a trip was perfect. It was the summer before Kaylea's senior year and Sophie's last year in middle school. The Bryan Family *Millennium Falcon*—a white, 2008 Kia Sedona van with 180,000 miles on it—had made multiple cross-country road trips and was in good condition for another adventure.

In the winter of 2016, I worked on a one-of-a-kind project with Baseball Seams Company combining both art and story—*America at the Seams*. My job was to interview people in every state, asking them their baseball stories with the goal of writing a coffee-table book. Because of that project, there were people all across this country I wanted to one day meet in person and play catch with. Part of the design of the trip was to see how many friends from *America at the Seams* we could find along the way.

Jamie and I planned a ten-day, six-state, 1,800-mile catch-playing tour of the Midwest, connecting with friends and strangers.

Kansas City, Missouri.

Overland Park, Kansas.

Omaha, Nebraska.

Sioux Falls, South Dakota.

Wallingford, Iowa.

Quad Cities, Iowa.

Rockford, Illinois.

Chicago, Illinois.

Plotted on a map, the itinerary looked somewhat like a heart.

I called the trip the Catch 365 Tour of Hope. Baseball Seams Company pitched in to sponsor it. As the day neared for departure, however, I had extreme doubts. I worried about the toll of the miles on the van and dreaded having to make any repairs on the road. The very thought of spending so much time in a van sounded exhausting. I feared Kaylea and Sophie would be bored to tears and Jamie would be perpetually frustrated with me. We had several family conversations around the dinner table and decided to go on an adventure. Living a good story means having the courage not only to dream big but to follow through with it. We entrusted the care of pets to family members and headed north to Kansas City.

Kauffman Stadium, the fountain-filled home of the Kansas City Royals, was the first stop on the tour. There I met Brett and four-year-old Bo Kesinger (day #145). Brett was named after the best Royals player ever, the only Royals player with a plaque in the National Baseball Hall of Fame. Brett named his oldest son after the best athlete ever to put on a Royals uniform, the two-sport athlete who ran on walls and ran through defensive lines. I've met George Brett twice and worked with Bo Jackson's agent on a children's book project. I've played catch with neither Brett nor Jackson. Yet.

Within the last year, the Kesingers learned that Bo has dyspraxia of the body and apraxia of speech.

"Basically, things that are pretty much intuitive for us are like a complicated dance routine for him," Brett said. "His speech is improving, but family interpretation is almost always necessary."

On the drive to the stadium, Bo told Brett, "Ethan is my best friend. He is a good friend." As soon as Brett parked their van, Bo hopped out with glove in hand and gave me a high five. "Hi, Ethan!" I understood him perfectly.

Brett greeted me with a hug and kiss, which I completely expected because that's who Brett is. Everyone needs someone like Brett in their lives, someone whose creations are inspiring and whose public displays of affection are always awkward. We walked across the parking lot to the space behind the jumbotron. Overnight rains had turned the grassy area into a marsh. I tipped my hat to the tributes to the 1985 and 2015 World Series champion teams posted on the back of the scoreboard. Within minutes, shoes and socks were saturated. Squish, squish, squish with every step. My toes felt like they were coated in jam. Bo didn't care one bit. He loved being outside and seemed to run forever.

The three of us quickly worked out a catch-playing rhythm. Brett and I spread out about ninety feet and tossed the ball. When Bo got close, he'd throw me the ball—left-handed—and I'd throw it back. He would then run to Brett and do the same thing. We were able to get in three or four throws in the time it took for Bo to run between us.

"I'm not really doing much in the way of creating art," Brett said. I tried not to let the disappointment show on my face.

⚾ ⚾ ⚾

When our drinking water had vanished and Bo seemed to melt into the grass, we ended the game of catch. Ten minutes later, Brett texted me a picture of Bo passed out in his car seat.

"The results of playing catch."

While looking through the pictures of Brett and Bo from our game of catch, trying to decide which ones to post on my blog, I got sidetracked and started looking through Brett's old artwork. Because Brett had three kids under five and a full-time youth-ministry position at his church, I could understand why Brett's art had taken a back seat. But it didn't make me happy. It took me a few minutes to put words to my disappointment.

Brett's art radiates whimsical joy and hope. From the very first illustration I saw on that napkin to his works celebrating creation and play, Brett's art not only puts a smile on my face but strengthens my faith, as well as challenges me to look for ways to help my neighbor. Because of Bo's challenges, Brett and his wife have worked diligently and patiently to help him be his best. Sometimes, being a parent means laying aside your dreams for the good of your child. Because Bo has two involved and loving parents, I am confident his future is bright and filled with countless days of running and playing catch. As he and his family persevere through this trial, I know Brett's life and faith will be all the richer.

⚾ ⚾ ⚾

My daughter Sophie is an artist. She started drawing when her hair was ringlet-curly and her smile was dominated by puffy cheeks. She gripped pencils and markers and crayons with her whole hand, a fist filled with creative intent, studying her subjects as she drew them. I know I am biased, but her drawings always have connected with me just like Brett's do. I was visiting with an artist friend, showing off the latest of Sophie's creations. The friend told me, "I can tell she's exploring techniques she's never been taught. Your job as a parent is to make certain she is always creating, to keep her exploring. Her art makes an incredible statement."

As a birthday gift, Sophie was given her first charcoal set and used it to create a piece symbolizing Catch 365. It was while I was studying her drawing that I realized that playing catch is living art.

Catch is a dance of connection and conversation and creativity between two partners. Everyone starts by imitating the greats and growing into their own style, feeling their way to express themselves through the strengths and limitations of their bodies. Catch is not just the basis for baseball, it is its own form of communication. Words don't need to be spoken.

And then I realized that all forms of play are living art.

It seems to me that play is an audacious act of hope. In a world that is driven by the bottom line and uber-efficiency, play loudly challenges everyone not to take themselves so seriously. Play breathes into our broken world and extends an invitation to join the present beauty.

Play creates margin in the midst of the mundane, offering fresh perspectives and insight in exchange for an investment of time.

Like art, like music, like love, play is a beautiful and exhausting act of hope. May we have the courage to live our lives as play-filled masterpieces.

7
Virdon's Values

Never let the fear of striking out keep
you from playing the game.
—*Babe Ruth*

There is a statue of Bill Virdon at the Missouri Sports Hall of Fame celebrating his unforgettable catch in the 1960 World Series. In the fourth inning of the first game, quotable Yankees catcher Yogi Berra blasted a drive to deep right-center field.

"I heard Clemente yelling something, but I wasn't sure. Going back, I felt that it was going to be tough to catch, but I also felt that I had a chance. I caught the ball up high, over my shoulder, and stepped on Roberto's foot as I bumped into the wall," Bill said.

His catch even has its own baseball card, titled "Virdon Saves Game." I keep a copy of the baseball card on my writing desk, right next to his autographed baseball. The catch preserved the lead for the Pirates, who went on to win the game, 6–4, and later the series.

Bill Virdon is one of the great faces of baseball in Missouri. In 1955, he was the National League Rookie of the Year playing for the

St. Louis Cardinals. The next spring, he was traded to the Pittsburgh Pirates. Shirley, his wife, learned about the trade listening to a pocket radio in the hospital, trying to entertain their daughter as she waited for the doctors to take the daughter back for a tonsillectomy. Playing for the Pirates, Virdon won the World Series in 1960 and the Gold Glove Award in 1962. He's coached dozens of professional outfielders, managed several teams, and won Manager of the Year in both leagues, with the New York Yankees in 1974 and with the Houston Astros in 1980. He's also managed several players now in the National Baseball Hall of Fame: Nolan Ryan, Roberto Clemente, Phil Niekro, Tim Raines, and Willie Stargell, as well as Pete Rose, Thurman Munson, and Lou Piniella.

While working on one baseball story, I reached out to the Virdons to see if Bill might have time for an interview. When he and his wife agreed to go to lunch with me, I was elated. At that lunch, he teased me over my love for the Royals and told me dozens of stories from baseball's golden era. Since that day, I have thoroughly enjoyed getting to know both Bill and Shirley. I was thrilled when Bill agreed to a game of catch (day #61).

"I tossed a ball some at spring training last year. Threw out a first pitch for the Springfield Cardinals a couple of years ago," Bill said.

At the age of eighty-six, Virdon is still quite active in the Springfield community, attending a variety of high school and collegiate sporting events. We chatted while Bill popped his fist into his glove, an old Rawlings with the leather worn through in multiple places and a couple of broken strings.

"I used to get a new glove every spring. I'd spend the year breaking it in, just playing catch, then use that glove the next season. This was one of my last gloves."

There is a storied beauty in old gloves.

We walked through the garage and out onto his back porch. Virdon flipped a baseball up in the air and straight into the sun. I know how to turn and use my glove to block the sun and catch the ball, but this ball was perfectly centered and I couldn't find it. At the last second, I ducked and covered my head. The ball fell to the ground right in front of me.

"Sorry," he said. "That was an accident. Had no idea the sun was right there."

"I thought you might be testing me."

"Oh, I'll test you all right. Scoot back," he said, motioning.

I stepped back ten feet.

"Farther."

Another few feet.

"Little farther."

Still another few feet.

"Good. Now put some zip on it."

Virdon played in the major leagues from 1955 through 1965 and then switched to coaching. Except for one month in 1968.

"Someone got injured, or maybe they were serving in the military, so they called me back up for a handful of games."

In 1968, Bill played in six games for the Pirates.

"I was just a late-game defensive replacement."

On July 23, Bill was put in as a pinch hitter for Dock Ellis in the bottom of the ninth inning. The Cincinnati Reds were winning 5–3. With one out and one on, Bill hit a game-tying home run.

"Only hit I had that season."

Because of his age, because he played in the days before social media, because he played for a rival team of the Cardinals, I think many people in southwest Missouri have forgotten just how good Bill Virdon was. His statue at the Missouri Sports Hall of Fame is a fitting tribute to his success in the game, both on and off the field.

There is a storied beauty in older ballplayers.

⚾ ⚾ ⚾

Sarah Davis and Ryan Landreth have organized multiple charity events on behalf of a friend who has cancer. The funds they raise help with treatment costs. They reached out to me and asked if I would be willing to play in one of their charity softball games.

I hesitated.

"It's been years since I played softball," I told Sarah.

"It's for a good cause," she replied.

I later learned that Sarah interpreted my confession of time passed as a statement of poor ability.

I am not a fan of slowpitch softball. I've got a pretty wicked scar on my right shin from stretching a double into a triple and sliding into third on a gravel infield. Cleaning up when I got home was not fun. I've got another scar on my knee from a time when I was playing shortstop during college on a team in South Carolina. Infields in South Carolina are more red clay than dirt. I slid on my leg to backhand a ball and stood up with a rock as big as a quarter sticking straight out from my kneecap. Cleaning that up was really not fun. When I lived in Kansas City, I played on a couple of church league teams, but for me, softball has never held anything close to the appeal of baseball.

After a couple of weeks of procrastinating and hem-hawing, I finally committed to the cause. I was most excited for the chance to play catch with Mike Engel (day #146). Years ago, Mike was the editor for a Royals-centric blog called *Kings of Kauffman*. He was the very first person who encouraged me to write Royals stories my way, filled not with statistics and detailed analytics but with stories of the intersection of all of life and baseball.[1] We texted several times as the day of the charity game grew nearer.

"I haven't hit or thrown or caught in quite a while," Mike said. "Probably not since I was coaching three years ago. I'm gonna fall apart inning by inning."

---

1   To read some of those stories, visit https://kingsofkauffman.com/author/ethanbryan/.

"It's been close to a decade since I last played in a real softball game," I replied. "Falling apart inning by inning is a distinct possibility. So is the horror of striking out."

"I hadn't even thought of that, but now I'm terrified of it."

The softball field park complex was across the Missouri state line and into Kansas. Jamie and Kaylea accompanied me to the fields and tried to stay cool in the sweltering, suffocating heat. The walk from the parking lot to the field was more than sufficient to warm up all of my muscles. No stretching was necessary.

A few years ago, The Weather Channel conducted a study and named Springfield, Missouri, the place of greatest weather variety. That means Springfield is the epicenter of "wait ten minutes and the weather will change." Over the course of a year, I experienced all of it. I played catch in wind chills that were double digits below zero and in heat indexes above 100, in the middle of snowstorms and thunderstorms and everything else except while the tornado sirens were sounding.

"What is there for you to gain from playing catch in the worst of weather?" a friend asked me.

Why do people race in the Iditarod or run ultramarathons? Why do people climb Mount Everest and dive to the depths of the oceans? Why do people eat seventy-four hot dogs in ten minutes?

To push themselves to an extreme, to the edge of suffering, to see what they can learn about life and themselves. The pure joy of setting a goal and overcoming adversity and obstacles in achieving that goal is exactly what it means to live a good story. To experience the cathartic joy of doing something hard and seeing it to completion.

I wore number 50 on Team Blue. I was the oldest player on Sarah's team and was scheduled to sub into the second half of the second game. *Late-game defensive replacement,* I told myself. I remembered comedian Brian Regan's baseball skit and laughed to myself as the innings passed. Even if I played only half of a game, Regan's skit assured me, I would still get a whole snow cone at the game's conclusion.[2] I was tempted to stick that snow cone down the back of my shirt or directly in my drawers.

Mike and I warmed up in right field, where the grass was high but dry, and kept an eye out for the line drives of teammates taking batting practice. Groans accompanied most of our throws, which was perfectly acceptable for warming up.

The game started and two players on Team Gold struck out in the first inning. Laughter and jeers abounded. Strikeouts are a part of the game, but the whole point of slowpitch softball is to put the ball in play. Striking out in slowpitch is beyond embarrassing. I made eye contact with Mike and raised my eyebrows.

"It happens," he said with a shrug.

Through the first five innings, Mike and I watched and cheered our team and did our best to keep muscles warm and stay hydrated. The keeping muscles warm part was easy. We were substituted into the game at the same time to play innings six through ten. Mike headed to second base and I went to right field. The whole time I was in the field, I hummed the song by Peter, Paul, and Mary:

> Right field, it's easy, you know.
> You can be awkward and you can be slow.
> That's why I'm here in right field
> just watching the dandelions grow.

The second batter in the top of the sixth inning was a power lefty for Team Gold. I moved back close to the warning track. The lefty hit a rocket shot to second base that Mike turned into a marshmallow and then easily threw to first for the out. I gave him a high five and said

---

2   See https://www.youtube.com/watch?v=EekMZDPEZ40.

a silent prayer of gratitude I wasn't playing second base. My defensive opportunity came the next inning.

I remember feeling like my feet were liquefying into the grass. Even though I wore sunscreen with an SPF somewhere north of 50, I was certain my skin was melting off my neck. The heat and humidity sapped all of my strength, my ability to move with any semblance of speed. Tan lines acquired during that game stayed with me the rest of the summer.

With two outs and a runner on first, a right-handed hitter for Team Gold stepped to the plate and swung at the first pitch. He hit a perfectly placed pop-up over Mike's head and into the triangle in between second base, right field, and right-center field. I broke for the ball on contact and started calling for it immediately.

"Ball! Ball! Ball! I got it!"

I tried to run hard, to run on a straight line to the ball. It felt like I was moving in slow motion, and I wasn't sure I would get to the ball in time. At the last second, I slid and crossed over my body with my left arm, holding my glove out in front of me with the palm up. I successfully snagged the ball before it hit the ground for the third out. Immediately, my feet felt swift and I had the energy of a dozen toddlers. I high-fived Mike on the jog into the dugout.

"Well, that most certainly did not suck!" Sarah greeted me.

"I didn't say I sucked. I just said it had been a really long time," I said, laughing.

Even if the catch wasn't statue-worthy, maybe some of Virdon's skills had rubbed off on me.

> Here in right field, it's important, you know.
> You gotta know how to catch,
> you gotta know how to throw.
> That's why I'm here in right field,
> just watching the dandelions grow!

I led off the bottom of the tenth inning and hit the ball solidly, but straight to the left fielder. Them's the breaks. Team Blue lost the game 17–13, but neither Mike nor I struck out. More important, between the two games and the more than seventy players involved, $2,000 was raised to help someone who could use a little hope in their life.

Even though softball isn't my sport, I loved being back on the field enjoying the camaraderie of a team and celebrating the success of teammates. Joining in the encouraging chatter in the dugout. Getting the chance to make a big play. Not striking out. It was the only game action I saw all year. Most of all, I was grateful for the opportunity to help someone else out through the sport.

⚾ ⚾ ⚾

When the Missouri Sports Hall of Fame dedicated Virdon's statue, his wife, Shirley, asked if they could use a poem I had written about him based on conversations he and I had had over the past couple of years. I was elated to be associated with the event.

Virdon's Values

I was fortunate
to do something
I really loved to do.
Be grateful
for every opportunity
to play ball.
Play the game the right way. Always.
Play hard and hustle. Always.
Be honest and fair. Always.
Be friendly and respectful to your teammates,
to the other team,

and to umpires. Always.
Remember people are watching you.
You are an example to someone. Always.
And love—really love!—
this game while you play.
One more thing.
Practice your swing using a pipe.
I did in the off-season.
Probably the smartest thing
I ever did as a player.

8
Do You Believe in Miracles?

"We're all human, aren't we? Every human
life is worth the same, and worth saving."
—KINGSLEY SHACKLEBOLT, HARRY POTTER
AND THE DEATHLY HALLOWS

"WE LIKE THE ROYALS. ME AND UNCLE E. WE DO." THE MIGHTY
Henry, my four-year-old nephew, is a quick learner.

Henry was born three months premature. He was so small he
could have fit in my glove. The first time I met him, while he was still
in the hospital, while he was still attached to feeding tubes, while he
was as frail as a hummingbird's whisper, Henry wore a stocking hat
designed to look like a baseball, which was adorable. Looking back at
his preemie pictures, I am reminded of the sacred fragility of life. His
oh-so-tiny heart flexing. His eyes wide in wonder. His muted squawks
and squeals.

Because Henry was born premature, all kinds of tests were run
on him. Through one of the tests, it was found that he had schizencephaly. Schizencephaly is an incredibly rare brain malformation

disorder occurring once in every 65,000 births. Henry has little splits or clefts in his brain positioned on the right side, squarely on the part controlling his gross and fine motor skills. Henry's manifestation of schizencephaly is a best-case scenario: the muscles on the left side of his body are extra tight, and he has occasional seizures.

Should Henry ever want to play baseball when he gets older, he most likely will have to catch and throw the ball with the same hand. Jim Abbott was born without a right hand and spent a decade pitching in the major leagues, hurling a no-hitter when he played for the New York Yankees. Nolan Ryan's grandson, Jackson, plays baseball in Texas. Because of cerebral palsy, he throws and catches with the same hand.

On the day I played catch with my sister (day #182), she wanted to learn how to play one-handed so she could teach Henry. I talked through the process: putting the ball in the glove on my right hand, flipping the ball out of the glove and into the air, dropping the glove, barehanding the ball, and then throwing it to Katy. Katy got the hang of the move almost immediately and then took it to the next level, pinning the glove to her body with her left arm after flipping the ball into the air. She repeated the motion several times before we called Dad out to film the effort on his phone, carefully preserving her talent for pride and posterity. I am amazed every time I watch it. I must be a good teacher.

It is because of Mighty Henry and my sister that I met SuperBo and the Macan family. Because of Henry's rare condition, when he was still quite young, Katy searched online for support groups and stories of others undergoing similar circumstances. Katy discovered the Macan family through such a support system.

"They live in Kansas and are Royals fans. Do you know them?" she asked via email.

I interpreted the question as, "Since they are Royals fans, you must know them."

Even though the Royals don't have a clue who I am, I am delighted to be associated with the team and its fan base. I imagine fans of other major league teams and teams of all sports have tight-knit communities of people who have connected through a shared love of the team. And the friends I have made while cheering for the baseball team in Kansas City are nothing short of amazing.

Like Sungwoo Lee, the superfan from South Korea.

Like Sarah and Ryan, who host charity softball games to cover medical expenses for someone with cancer.

Like Billy (day #364), who sold T-shirts and raised $1,500 to help pay for repairs at the Buck O'Neil Education and Research Center in Kansas City after it was vandalized and flooded. (But that's jumping ahead to the last chapter.)

Like John and Carolyn Macan and their children, Leksi, Johnny, Brookie, and Bo.

⚾ ⚾ ⚾

Named after Bo Jackson, Bo Macan has a disease so rare doctors are naming it after him: Bo syndrome. Bo has seen doctors at the National Institutes of Health who are confounded by the combination of symptoms his body displays. He takes sixteen medications to try to ease his suffering. An interesting twist to his story is that Bo has a twin sister, Brookie, who is perfectly healthy.

I read the story my sister sent me and felt compelled to get in touch with the family. In the first week of January 2016, I sent Carolyn, Bo's mom, a ridiculous email.

"So. I know this sounds weird, and I'm not exactly sure how to go about it, but what if I wrote Bo's story and then found an illustrator and then sold copies of the book to help with medical costs? Would you and your family and Bo have any interest in that?"

Carolyn replied faster than Cool Papa Bell ran the bases.[1]

"How in the world did you find us?"

Carolyn and I exchanged several emails, and on Mighty Henry's second birthday, the first draft of *They Call Me SuperBo* was completed. With significant editorial help and illustrations from Wilson Tharp, a senior graphic-design student at Missouri State University, the story became a fun children's book comparing Royals superstar Bo Jackson and his namesake, Bo Macan.

> Strength is more than just muscles. Strength is having the courage
> and the hope to face tomorrow, even if it's going to be hard.
> "Tomorrow is a new day," Mom always says.

I was put in touch with MLB lawyers in New York because we wanted to use the logos of the Royals. I was sent a contract full of legalese that took me quite some time to interpret. Eventually, we successfully negotiated a deal, my first and only major league deal: the book would have only one printing. Working with the Macan family on that project burned a dream deep in my heart to write books and tell stories of hope that raise money to help people in need.

⚾ ⚾ ⚾

Nathan Rueckert is the president and founder of Baseball Seams Company. For seventeen years, Nathan has been transforming old baseballs into art. Baseballs others deem unusable or trash, he is able

---

1   Cool Papa Bell is considered one of the fastest people ever to play baseball. "One time he hit a line drive right past my ear. I turned around and saw the ball hit him sliding into second," Satchel Paige once said of Bell. Bell played in the Negro Leagues during the days of segregated baseball and was elected to the National Baseball Hall of Fame in 1974.

to give second life as cuff links or a necklace or a keychain or an American flag.

In 2016, Nathan had the massive and audacious idea of creating a map of the United States out of baseballs, each state crafted from balls obtained from that state. The baseballs were connected to specific stories—stories of hope, healing, and baseball bringing people together. The goal was to represent all aspects of the game through the stories and illustrate how baseball is more than just a game.

Nathan gave me the once-in-a-lifetime opportunity to research and write the stories. It was one of the most overwhelming invitations I've ever received. I spent hundreds of hours trying to find state-specific stories and poured my heart into the extraordinary project. There is no other baseball project like *America at the Seams*—art and story centered around the greatest game to bring hope and encouragement to others.

After writing *They Call Me SuperBo,* I reconnected with the Macan family to write their story for *America at the Seams* as the representative story for the state of Kansas. Bo's older sister, Leksi, plays softball on her high school team, and her coach helped organize a home run derby fundraiser for the family. The community rallied around the event on a picture-perfect October afternoon, with T-shirts and food and a deejay and local media coverage. The whole Macan family is quite athletic, and everyone took swings to try to hit one over the fence. I also participated, and even though I didn't hit a home run, I also didn't swing and miss. Success.

When Jamie and I were planning the road trip through the Midwest, I wanted to find a way to reconnect with the Macans. Leksi's summer fastpitch softball team, the KC Fireballs, was in the middle of a massive Memorial Day tournament, with six games of pool play over the first two days. Leaving Kansas City on the way to Omaha, Nebraska, we drove to Leksi's tournament to play catch with her team (day #147).

I had just started the Bryan Family *Millennium Falcon* and was confirming directions with Jamie when Carolyn texted me, "Leksi hit one out!" It was the first time one of my catch partners hit a home run on the same day we played catch, but it wouldn't be the last.

⚾ ⚾ ⚾

From the age of three, Pam was Mom's best friend. Because of a farming accident, Pam's dad had a wooden leg. Mom used to tell me and my sister stories about Pam's dad's wooden leg. We were fascinated by it. Every single time we ate at Wendy's, we asked Mom to tell the story again. The dining room tables at Wendy's used to be covered in vintage newspaper ads. One of the ads was for a wooden leg. Whenever we ate at Wendy's, my sister and I raced around the dining room to find a table with a wooden leg and "win."

A few years ago, Kaylea was at one of her first practices for the worship team at church. I drove her there and stayed to listen. While the band rehearsed, I grabbed some coffee and bagels from the back of the sanctuary. The bagel table was an old table from Wendy's. I quickly found the wooden leg, took a picture—yes, flip phones take pictures—and sent it to my sister and Mom.

It was the ultimate win.

When the church moved locations, the youth minister gave me that table. I took it to Katy and Henry on one of our catch-playing trips to Arkansas.

Pam's daughter is Heather. Heather's oldest son is Beau. On Beau's thirteenth birthday, he was in Springfield for the first time, playing in a baseball tournament at Cooper Park. The park complex is only five minutes from my house, so I met Beau for catch (day #167) and told him the story about his great-grandfather's wooden leg. I asked if he had any birthday wishes.

"Win today. Win tomorrow. Win the tournament. And maybe hit one over the fence."

I made a deal with Beau: if he hit a bomb on his birthday, I'd send him a copy of *America at the Seams*.

In the bottom of the first inning, Beau stepped up to the plate with the bases loaded and promptly singled to left, driving in a run. He later scored in the ten-run first inning. Beau was the first hitter in the bottom of the second inning, and he slugged a high fly ball that sailed, like a baseball rainbow seeking its pot of gold, over the left-field fence. A birthday bomb, and I witnessed it.

That summer, both Leksi and Beau hit more home runs than I ever did over the course of my illustrious eight-year baseball career.

⚾ ⚾ ⚾

As soon as the Bryan Family *Millennium Falcon* pulled into the parking lot at Leksi's tournament, a man called out to me, "I see a SuperBo T-shirt!" The man was John Macan's dad, Bo's grandfather. Right next to the man was Bo. I didn't expect him to recognize me, so I reintroduced myself as the writer of his book. He gave me a smile and a high five. His grandpa said, "It's pretty hot out here today. He really needs some air conditioning." I understood completely.

It was hotter on day #147 than on day #146, and heat in the Midwest means humidity and a steady stream of sweat dripping from the bill of my hat along with an overwhelming desire not to move a single muscle. This kind of heat is usually reserved for mid-August and back to school, not Memorial Day and end of school. This kind of heat tests air-conditioning units in homes and vehicles and melts the soles of shoes on parking lots. This kind of heat is best for napping on beaches and splashing in pools or hiding in movie theaters. It's not the kind of heat for being in open-air ballparks surrounded by asphalt lots.

Carolyn met me and my family at the gates and walked us back to the team. She had already told them about Catch 365, which had to have been a hilarious conversation. I imagined the ballplayers reacting with eye rolls and head shakes to the idea of playing catch after having already played five games in solid black uniforms. I wouldn't have blamed them one bit. As Leksi's teammates grabbed their gloves, I warmed up with Leksi and congratulated her on hitting a home run. Her teammates slowly joined in playing catch, including Sami, who had torn her meniscus and ACL and had surgery scheduled for after the tournament's conclusion. I commiserated with her, telling my own torn ACL surgery story. Sophie asked to borrow one of Leksi's gloves and also participated in what turned out to be a fun eleven-person, full-of-laughter, who-cares-how-hot-it-is game of catch.

Thoroughly saturated in sweat, my family said our goodbyes and wished the KC Fireballs luck in their next game. We climbed back into the van, turned a movie on, and started the journey north.

⚾ ⚾ ⚾

I do not know why Henry was born with schizencephaly.

I do not know why Bo was born with Bo syndrome even as his twin sister was perfectly healthy.

Humans are so quick to compare and judge themselves deficient. We compare our weaknesses to others' strengths and wish we had been born with their gifts and abilities and bodies. I wish I could throw a baseball like Jim Abbott or Nolan Ryan. I wish I had a 100 mph fastball or an impossible-to-catch knuckleball or a curveball that buckles batters' knees. Am I less than, deficient, because I don't?

In the process of writing *America at the Seams,* I loved listening to strangers share their baseball stories. Each story was an original. Each story was a masterpiece. The lessons I learned through the writing of *America at the Seams* were reflected in how I approached my daily catch partners.

Every single person was an original.

Every single person was a masterpiece.

Every single person was a miracle.

Henry is a miracle.

Bo is a miracle.

Beau and Leksi and Pam and Heather and Carolyn and John and Sophie and Kaylea and Jamie all are miracles. Using the word miracle on a regular basis does not minimize the foundational miracles of faith. Using the word miracle reminds me of the nearness of God in the middle of the ordinary, boring, monotonous rhythms of everyday life. Using the word miracle is a humble acknowledgment that I don't know everything and that I am not in control. Using the word miracle celebrates the original masterpiece of every person on the planet.

We see what we expect to see. Maybe if we expected to see miracles every day, we would see glimpses small and large of unexpected grace and wonder. We would see the people who share life with us day in and day out.

From day one, Henry has had a phenomenal team of therapists and teachers, along with his parents, working with him, praying for him, and playing with him. They are miracle workers, those whose touch and wisdom give Henry strength and direction. The same is true for Bo. His family and friends are miracle workers. His parents and siblings all have made sacrifices time and time again so Bo can be his best.

Every superhero has an origin story. For a few years now, I have followed the Macans' journey through the highs and lows of surviving and living with a loved one who has his own syndrome. I believe they are a family of superheroes.

9
Why Baseball?

But it all comes down to friendship,
treating people right.
—*ERNIE BANKS*

"WHY DO YOU CARE SO MUCH ABOUT BASEBALL? IT'S JUST A GAME."

Throughout the catch-playing year, I was asked this question hundreds of times. Why baseball? Why not politics or medicine or law? Why not cars or camping or hunting? Why not something that makes a difference in this world?

If you had asked me this question when I was eight, I would have answered, "Because it's fun. It's fun playing catch with Dad, and it's fun hitting the ball and running the bases and sliding. Baseball is fun." When you're eight years old, fun is the highest priority.

As we age, we forget for some reason how important fun is in keeping brains and bodies healthy. The stresses of daily life distract us and fun gets pushed farther and farther down the list of priorities. For some people, unfortunately, fun gets forgotten.

If you had asked me this question when I was fifteen, I would have

answered, "Because I'm going to play for the Kansas City Royals."
It's how I answered the "Where are you going?" part of Mr. Nichols'
question. Playing baseball professionally was my dream. I attended a
summer camp around the age of ten and met a former minor league
player. He said, "Do you know the odds of anyone in this camp playing professionally? Maybe one, possibly two of you will have any kind
of baseball future after high school." Encouragement wasn't really his
forte. For the remainder of the camp, the group of boys I was with
fought to prove which of us was the chosen one. None of us made it.

My dream of playing baseball professionally kept me invested in
school. I wanted to be recognized as a "student athlete." My last game,
however, took place in the summer of 1991. At sixteen years old, I had
yet to hit my growth spurt; I was the smallest player on my team by far.
I couldn't throw as hard or run as fast as my teammates. My coach told
me I made the junior varsity team more for my heart than my skills.
I always thought that statement was a compliment. At the end of the
season, I reasoned that people who played professionally were more
talented than I was. I didn't know that making dreams come true is
about having the tenacious courage not to quit when it's really hard.

I gave up on my dream far too easily. To this day, quitting ball is
one of my biggest regrets.

But I always knew where my glove was.

And playing catch with two people who worked in professional
baseball helped me discover my answer to that oft-asked question.

⚾ ⚾ ⚾

In March, my cousin Paul and his family were in Springfield for a
basketball tournament with his older son, Nathan. His younger son,
Caleb, helped the team by recording the games, providing me with
entertaining and insightful commentary whenever the camera was
paused. Caleb wanted to be on the court. He wanted the chance to

strut his stuff and help the team win. But he wasn't old enough. We screamed and yelled and applauded and stomped our way through a double-overtime thriller that ended in a heartbreaking loss.

Earlier that same March day, while waiting for the next round of basketball games, Caleb agreed to a game of catch (day #72). Because he is the second-born son with four other siblings, two of whom were adopted and one who has cystic fibrosis, I feared Caleb's dreams and desires might get overlooked. We played catch so I could hear his story. At that time I had no idea that later in the year, my family would make a trip to Omaha, where Paul's family lives, so I lightheartedly tweeted a nomination for Caleb to throw out a first pitch at an Omaha Storm Chasers game in honor of Catch 365.

The Omaha Storm Chasers are the Minor League Triple-A affiliate team of the Kansas City Royals. Martie Cordaro, president and general manager of the Storm Chasers, replied to the tweet almost immediately.

"Done."

In Minor League Baseball, creative team names abound: Richmond Flying Squirrels, Albuquerque Isotopes, Jacksonville Jumbo Shrimp. The league also does a remarkable job of engaging and entertaining fans through innovative theme nights: Harry Potter Night, Star Wars Night, Edgar Allan Poe Bobblestache Night. I think all minor league teams could use a catch-playing mascot.

After playing catch with the Macans, my family drove to Omaha on the day of a record high temperature—101 degrees. Thankfully, the air-conditioner in the van was excellent. I finally made it to my first Storm Chasers game. Before the game, the Storm Chasers invited fans to play catch on the outfield grass. Not one blade of grass was out of place. It looked like a Bob Ross painting. It was so picture perfect, one of my cousin's daughters thought it was fake. My family participated in the catch-playing event and was joined by Paul and Nathan and Caleb and several of Caleb's friends, because it was also the night for his first pitch as a special guest of the team.

"Nervous?" I asked.

"Yeah, and excited," he replied with a happy-go-lucky smile.

From jitters and increased heartrate to sweaty palms and coursing adrenaline, the body processes the feelings of nervousness and excitement in almost exactly the same way. Casting nervousness in the positive light of excitement is profoundly wise self-talk. I was invited on the field to stand on the warning track and watch Caleb walk to the mound for his pitch. I was as excited as if I were throwing out the first pitch myself. He took a breath, wound up slowly, and threw a strike. A smile exploded across his face. He walked back to the track and I greeted him with a high five.

We sat in left field for the game, skin sticking to seats and sweat streaming from every pore, refilling our water bottles almost every inning. I immediately recognized the Storm Chasers' left fielder—Paulo Orlando. Paulo Orlando made his major league debut for the Royals in early 2015, becoming only the third Brazilian-born player to make it all the way to the pros. Paulo was the first player in MLB history to triple for his first three base hits, quickly earning the nickname Paulo Triple-O. That fall, he won the World Series with the Royals. Every time Paulo took the field and every time he exited, I yelled at the top of my lungs, "Let's go, Paulo!" In the sixth inning, he acknowledged my obnoxious yells and pointed in my direction.

In a four-game series against the Round Rock Express, the game we saw was the only one the Storm Chasers lost. You can't win 'em all.

The next morning, I went back to Werner Park to meet Martie Cordaro for the fourth day of the catch-playing Tour of Hope (day #148). Martie has been with the team since 2007 and was the Baseball America Minor League Executive of the Year in 2013. He's also a former professional drummer and a huge Star Wars fan and had plans to see *Solo* after the midday game.

I first visited with Martie while researching stories for *America at the Seams*. I heard a Storm Chasers story I thought might be the perfect representative for the state of Nebraska. Miles Mortensen, the four-year-old son of Omaha Storm Chasers reliever Clayton Mortensen, had been battling stage 4 neuroblastoma since age two. The Storm Chasers supported Miles and Clayton and the whole Mortensen family by hosting a Super Miles night with specially designed jerseys.

"The idea was Brian Duensing's," Martie said. "He'd only been with the Royals for a few months, and now he was doing something to help a teammate he hadn't known all that long."

I remembered the Super Miles night because Royals star outfielder Alex Gordon was in Omaha on a rehabilitation assignment. I thought about bidding on his jersey, but it quickly surpassed my budget. I wore my Gordon T-shirt to play catch with Martie.

I reintroduced myself to Martie, and as a thank-you for his time, I gave him a copy of another book I'd written, *Run Home and Take a Bow*. Brett Kesinger's cover art made it look like an oversized baseball card featuring a miniature Alex Gordon. Martie ran the book to his office and returned with a Jarrod Dyson bobblehead. Inadvertently I had successfully negotiated my first trade with a minor league team before we even played catch.

⚾ ⚾ ⚾

Dan Reiter is the general manager of the Springfield Cardinals, the Double-A affiliate of the parent organization in St. Louis. His baseball story is fascinating. In 2004, after graduating from the University of Missouri with a degree in marketing, Dan entered a Fox Sports TV contest by submitting a VHS tape displaying his Cardinals super-fandom. The lucky winner of the contest would be given the opportunity to be president of the St. Louis Cardinals for a day.

Dan won.

After winning the contest, Dan was delighted to spend a couple of days in St. Louis, meeting and visiting with then-president of the St. Louis Cardinals, Mark Lamping. That series of events, from winning the contest to meeting the president, helped solidify Dan's dreams of working in professional baseball.

From the very first day of its operation in 2005, Dan has been with the Springfield team, beginning his career by working in the front office in a sales capacity. His first three seasons, Dan was an account executive, then he was promoted to senior account executive for another three seasons. Dan continued to succeed and advance within the front office: corporate sales manager, manager of corporate partnerships, director of sales and marketing, vice president of sales and marketing, vice president, and ultimately, general manager.

Over the years, I have chosen to be ignorant of the business side of baseball, thinking I would better enjoy the game as a fan. Dan is convinced his passion for the game as a fan helps him make better business decisions. On a stormy spring day, we played catch in the indoor training facility next to Hammons Field (day #123), and Dan gave me an education on the structure of the front office and the interaction between the Double-A team and the MLB team.

"Baseball is teaching me that everyone needs to have more fun. In general, we need to lighten up and work on having more fun," Dan said. But even fun takes serious work. "No one in the front office gets a real off-season. The preparation and work we do from October through March set the standard for the next season."

If I were the general manager, I would want to shag fly balls during batting practice. I would do it for exercise and for fun. For those outfielders who use batting practice to work on their skills, I wouldn't get in the way. But Dan is not even tempted by the opportunity.

"I have great respect for the athletes on the field," he said. "This game is their profession. I don't want my presence to take away from the importance of their preparation and work."

If I were the general manager of a minor league team, anytime a major league player made an appearance on a rehabilitation assignment, I would be quick to introduce myself and ask for an autograph. I wouldn't dare sell or auction the autographs but would preserve them along with scorecards of that player's game as simple documentation of friends made through the game.

"I work in baseball because I absolutely love this game," Dan said, "but several times you have to step back and remove the fan from the businessperson. I want the players I interact with to respect me as a businessperson. I don't ask for autographs, period. I introduce myself and ask how we can best serve and help them while they are with us. My favorite players are the ones who talk to and sign autographs for the fans. I cheer for the players who are kind to our fans and thankful to those who come out to support them."

If I were the general manager of a minor league team, toward the end of each season, I would create a Player for a Day contest. The winner would sign a contract with the team and get their own uniform and sit on the bench during the game. This person could be male or female, almost any age above eighteen. Their salary would be donated to a nonprofit organization of their choice. If it was a late-season game and the outcome couldn't affect the standings, the person would get to play for a half inning or more.

"The best part of my job is the people," Dan said. "I love the people. From that first season to today, I have made amazing friends. I love seeing people smile in this ballpark. I love that what we do helps thousands of people create strong memories with friends and family."

⚾ ⚾ ⚾

It takes a community effort to support a baseball team at any level. Front-office staff, field crew, concessions staff, broadcast and media crew, medical and training staff, and others put in thousands of behind-the-scenes hours so the fans can best enjoy their experience.

Like Dan, Martie works in baseball, but he doesn't play the game. We spread out in front of the Storm Chasers' dugout in foul territory for our game of catch. I resisted every single urge to run out to the mound and practice throwing my own first pitch. Martie takes the same approach to the game and his work as general manager as Dan does. He's not out chasing down fly balls during batting practice or stepping into the cages to take swings. He's not coaching the players to make adjustments or giving signs to the manager. Martie uses his position to give back to the greater Omaha community.

"The best part of being a GM is seeing people, fans and players, making memories at the ballpark."

I will remember the twenty-odd people who came out to watch Caleb's first pitch for a long time. Getting a chance to run around in center field and play catch is another memory I'll cling to, as well as the ever-so-brief acknowledgment from Paulo.

⚾ ⚾ ⚾

Like playing catch, baseball is a game of relationships, connecting people to one another, to generations past and generations future.

I remember going to the 2014 ALCS games with Dad and screaming until I lost my voice when the Royals won to advance to the World Series for the first time in twenty-nine years.

I remember attending the Royals' annual Dressed to the Nines games with Kaylea, games that are a tribute to the Negro Leagues and a fundraiser for the Negro Leagues Baseball Museum. In 2015, not only did we cheer the Royals as they shut out the Yankees, but because we were wearing our Sunday best, we were also invited on to the pregame show as well.

I remember taking a baby Kaylea to a Royals game with my mom and discovering how much Kaylea hated the victory fireworks.

I remember going to the next-to-the-last home game of the season with Sophie in 2015 and hearing her prophetic prediction: "The Royals are gonna win the last game of the season." She was right. I even wrote a poem about that game.

I remember going to a Toledo Mud Hens game with Grandma Bryan and to 1986 spring training in Florida with my family and taking my first youth group in Texas to watch the Rangers play the Royals. The Royals won.

Those who work in baseball value people, and one of the most treasured and important gifts you can give to people is a good memory. Over and over again, playing catch created exactly this kind of memory.

⚾ ⚾ ⚾

After spending time with baseball professionals Dan and Martie, I found the words to answer the question so many catch partners asked. Now if you ask me, "Why baseball?" this is how I will answer.

Baseball is a game of failure. This is the standard answer. But as a recovering perfectionist, I've found that learning how to experience failure and move forward is a good thing. Our culture is obsessed with overnight-success stories. We need to be reminded that failure is neither fatal nor final, just a necessary step for accruing wisdom. Failure can be part of the fun.

Baseball is a reminder of just how little control we have over anything. Fans cannot control whether their favorite team will win any more than the hitter can control the outcome once the ball is put into play. Do your best in that moment, regardless of the outcome. Breathe deeply and enjoy the experience, living into the fullness of the moment.

In baseball, you are not alone. You take the field and play as a team who, if you're lucky, will love and support you like family through the highs and lows of a season. This world could use more of a team mentality in daily life, especially if we could learn to see that we're all on the same team. When our teammates struggle, we've got their backs, through the highs and lows of life.

When I first started playing catch with Dad, it was about chasing baseball dreams. Playing catch back then was a way to sharpen my skills and practice all things related to the game—fielding pop-ups and grounders and throwing fastballs and curveballs. I treasure all my memories of playing catch with Dad.

On New Year's Day, playing catch was something quirky and odd to share with my daughters, a chance to laugh and make a memory in the freezing weather. It transformed into an adventure all about people, an adventure of creating strong memories with family and friends new and old.

⚾ ⚾ ⚾

Thunder rumbled and lightning flashed and a steady rain fell as I drove home after spending time with Dan. When I got home, I discovered I had a message from Nathan Rueckert.

"Fun testimonial today!"

Nathan had forwarded a message from William O. DeWitt III, current president of the St. Louis Cardinals.

"Baseball has been passed down through the generations in America, and has created countless memories for families and friends with its traditions and exciting action. The inspirational stories in this book, paired with Nathan's meaningful artwork, remind us that the game has been a constant in the history of our changing country. *America at the Seams* has beautifully captured the essence of how baseball is more than just a game."

Writing the stories of all my catch partners on a blog was a blessing. I'll treasure rereading the stories and the memories of the year of playing catch for the rest of my life.

10

Southpaw Stories

All men dream: but not equally. Those who dream
by night in the dusty recesses of their minds wake in
the day to find that it was vanity: but the dreamers
of the day are dangerous men, for they may act their
dreams with open eyes, to make it possible. This I did.
—*T. E. LAWRENCE*

THE SAME YEAR I MOVED TO SPRINGFIELD FROM GRAND JUNCTION, Colorado, on the first day of the month in which I was born, Hank Aaron and Frank Robinson were inducted into the National Baseball Hall of Fame. I learned about the quaint, lakeside village of Cooperstown, New York, and the phenomenal careers of the Home Run King along with the 1966 Triple Crown winner. Both men played the game with fierce, competitive passion and carried themselves with class on and off the field.

Bronze plaques of baseball immortals line oak walls behind massive marble columns in the Plaque Gallery inside the brick building of the Hall of Fame. Almost everyone who plays the game and dreams of stepping onto a major league field has, at one point or another, entertained thoughts of being inducted into the Hall of Fame as one of the best. Reading the stories of Hank Aaron and Frank Robinson stirred my Hall of Fame dreams.

⚾ ⚾ ⚾

Nathan Rueckert, the artist behind the Baseball Seams Company, lives in Sioux Falls, South Dakota. God has a goofy sense of humor locating a baseball company in a place where winter thrives six months each year. Nathan is convinced every baseball tells a story, holds a memory, and has the potential to bring people together. When he asked me to write stories for *America at the Seams,* it was one of the few times, like when Bob invited me to the *Field of Dreams* movie site, that I've answered with a resounding yes before thinking through all the details and implications of my decision. I knew from the start I wanted to be part of this extraordinary project and am grateful Nathan offered me the chance to contribute my words. I am convinced there is no other baseball project like this—art and story centered around the greatest game to bring hope and encouragement to others. I wrote the stories and Nathan stitched together the states.

⚾ ⚾ ⚾

After leaving Omaha, on yet another day of oppressive heat during our catch-playing Tour of Hope, my family headed to Sioux Falls to find Nathan for a game of catch. Nathan suggested Falls Park, an iconic Sioux Falls venue full of the scenery and history of the roaring waterfalls. Now a baseball artist and banker, Nathan was a left-handed pitcher at Truman State University in Kirksville, Missouri. It was while he was a student that he created the first Baseball Seams Company art, a replica of the United States flag using baseball leather and seams for the stripes and a swath from his practice jersey for the blue patch of stars. He titled it *America's Game*. He has made many versions of it based on the original design, and they have hung across the country, including in the White House while George W. Bush was president.

I love playing catch with southpaws. They can't throw the ball straight. Not that people who throw the ball right-handed always throw it straight, but there is something about the way lefties throw the ball that imparts a nigh physics-defying spin and makes it do fun and unusual things. There is a reason baseball created the term "crafty lefty"—a designation for someone who doesn't necessarily throw hard but has incredible movement on their pitches and pinpoint control. There really isn't an equivalent for righties. If there were, maybe I could have kept playing ball. And lefties who can hit 100 mph on the radar gun also catch the attention of scouts and teams, even if they are older than traditional ballplayers.

⚾ ⚾ ⚾

In the fall of 2017, just after the start of the MLB postseason and before Sophie's birthday, I was invited to write poems as part of Missouri State University's creative writing club's fundraiser for Ozarks Literacy Council, a nonprofit organization that provides free literacy tutoring. Inside Siceluff Hall, I quietly sat at the end of a white folding table while talkative, extroverted tablemates half my age tried to convince passersby of their need to donate a dollar in exchange for a poem. I had committed to writing for three hours, which included a changing of the tablemate guard. Once I tired of writing haiku, without any pressing poems to write for paying patrons, I engaged my new tablemate in conversation, asking ridiculous question after ridiculous question and answering her questions in return.

For some unexplainable reason, I asked her, "Have you ever seen the movie *The Rookie?*"

The expression on her face dramatically changed. At first, I assumed it was because she was so young she had never heard of the movie. And then I wondered if she'd misheard me, and I tried to think of other phrases that might sound like "the rookie" and could be construed as offensive. She reached for her backpack, unzipped it, and rummaged through it.

"It's been a hard couple of weeks," she said. "So I went to the library and checked this out."

She pulled out a well-worn DVD of the movie.

"It's my favorite movie, the one I always turn to whenever I need an encouraging word. I've watched it every day this week after class."

In my backpack was a copy of a novel I'd written, *Dreamfield,* which was endorsed by Jim "The Rookie" Morris. "Ethan takes us on an incredible journey to his past. In the process, he learns the important life—and baseball—lessons of never giving up on a dream, being present in your life, and allowing God and your faith to carry you through. This is a must-read!"

I'd printed off the email with his endorsement and carried it around in my back pocket for weeks, until I accidentally left it there and washed the jeans and shredded his words. I handed the book to my tablemate and told her to look at the back cover.

"The Rookie endorsed your book?" she asked.

For the next hour, our conversation took on a different tone. Because we each connected to Jim Morris's story, we were able to talk openly and honestly about all aspects of life. People find hope when they see someone who could be their coworker, their neighbor, or even their friend chase their dreams and accomplish the seemingly impossible.

At thirty-five, an age when ballplayers start contemplating retirement, Jim broke into the major leagues and pitched for the Tampa Bay Devil Rays. On September 18, 1999, he made his debut and struck out the first hitter he faced on four fastballs. (The third one was fouled off.) Disney made a movie of his story starring Dennis Quaid. Jim made his acting debut as "Orlando Umpire #2." I cannot count the number of times I've seen the movie. It's one of those movies that, when it's on TV, I'll stop channel surfing and watch until it's over.

In May 2018, on a day of baby-blue skies and pollen-coated cars, on day #130, I drove to Kansas City to visit Jim, who now travels the country as a motivational speaker, encouraging and empowering people as they strive to make their dreams a reality. I can't imagine how many thousands of times he's told his story, but as he told it to me, I could feel hope welling within. After visiting with him, I wanted to do something epic.

Just beyond the right-field fence, in a tree-lined grass patch, we played catch and I secretly hoped some of Jim's dream-chasing baseball mojo might rub off on me. To this day, I continue to hold strong to my ridiculous baseball aspirations. My dream has been the same for the last forty years of my life—to play baseball for the Kansas City Royals. If anyone could give me pointers about making that dream come true, Jim had to be the expert.

Jim is also a southpaw. He used his glove that, along with his jersey, was on display at Cooperstown for six months. I loved watching the tight spins on his breaking pitches and the life and movement he had on his four-seam fastball. He gave me a major league education on throwing a knuckle curveball and a split-finger change, and adjusted my slider grip and release point.

"Life is a grind, just like the baseball season," Jim said. "If you think you're beat, then you are. The key is to choose hope. As long as you still hold on to hope, almost anything is possible."

Chasing dreams takes a little bit of crazy, a lot of courage, and every bit of never-give-up one can muster.

"Life is never going to stop throwing things at you," he said. "How you choose to react determines whether you grow or give up. God took me, the person least likely to be a speaker, and turned me into a storyteller. For anyone who hears my story, I want to encourage them to find ways to give to those around them. You gain so much more when you learn to give. I hope that's what people take away from my story."[1]

Southpaw stories, like life and chasing dreams, are rarely straight.

⚾ ⚾ ⚾

"They used to say I was throwing off-speed stuff in Little League, which was against the rules, but I wasn't," Nathan said as we played on day #149. "It was just my fastball had good life."

With the roar of the waterfalls behind me, Nathan threw a couple of fantastic curveballs that dropped right off the table as they neared. Even his normal throws had movement. Nothing was straight. When I was in eighth grade, I did a science-fair project on the physics of a curveball. I would have received a better grade if Nathan had given live demonstrations. I tried my best to impress him with a knuckleball, but it was horrible. I saw several people pointing at us as we played catch near the falls, which I took as a compliment, though no one asked if they could join in.

After catch, my family toured the falls and downtown Sioux Falls, walking along the fun sculpture walk. We found Baseball Seams Company headquarters, where the map is displayed in the window surrounded by an assortment of baseball cards. We took family pictures, and Kaylea and Sophie and Jamie finally got to see what I had worked on with Nathan for two years. Turning dreams into reality requires silencing interior doubt-and-fear-filled monologues and pouring one's heart into disciplined, persevering, consistent hard work.

⚾ ⚾ ⚾

---

1   Read more of Jim's amazing story at jimtherookiemorris.com.

At her preschool graduation, when asked what she wanted to do when she grew up, Kaylea said she wanted to play violin in her daddy's band. I know the power of music to bring hope and heal the broken places within. Because I am convinced music is truly a divine language, even though I no longer have my own band, I have done everything I can to encourage Kaylea's musical dreams. As she started her senior year in high school, we visited multiple colleges so she could tour campuses and participate in violin auditions. When we made a day trip to tour the University of Central Arkansas, I took my gloves and spent time with the head baseball coach.

Coach Allen Gum played baseball at Crowder College in Neosho, Missouri, as both a pitcher and an outfielder. Coach Gum has been at UCA for more than eight years and is the winningest coach in UCA history. His coaching tenure is full of stories of epic postseason wins as well as beating some of the best NCAA baseball programs, including Missouri State, Oklahoma State, and Mississippi State. Three of Coach Gum's players were drafted by the Kansas City Royals in 2018: pitcher Tyler Gray, catcher William Hancock, and outfielder Hunter Strong. The program also celebrated its first player in the big leagues—Jonathan Davis of the Toronto Blue Jays, who got his first big-league hit against southpaw David Price. Coach Gum is another southpaw who encourages chasing after dreams and working at it with everything you've got.

Kaylea and I parked by the baseball field, and Coach Gum and his family were the first people to welcome us to campus. Not wanting to waste any time, I grabbed a glove and started walking out onto the artificial-turf infield, which had survived the rains of recent days.

"I look for players with grit, who maybe got the shine knocked off of them at junior college," Coach Gum told me as we warmed up (day #310). "They need to be tough and truly love playing this game. It's harder here; we don't have a lot of the facilities that other programs have. We look for those players we feel like the other schools might have overlooked. Players who make other players better. Players who give energy to their teammates."

Coach Gum threw beautiful sliders and knuckleballs and even complimented the strength of my arm. He gave me a couple of fun practice toys to help sharpen the run on my two-seam fastball.

Before we left for Kaylea's campus tour, Coach Gum told us about the tradition he uses to develop camaraderie among the team. Using marbles as a reminder of how many games are in the season, one player is chosen to receive a marble after each game as a personal trophy based on values determined by Coach Gum.

"We count out marbles for all of our guaranteed game days; we know we're not promised the postseason. Our senior players gift the marbles to underclassmen who work to earn them. I get a good idea of the feel and potential for the team by how they treat the marbles. I still receive messages from former players who know exactly where their marbles are."

Coach Gum stressed the power and importance of a game of catch. How playing catch with a parent or an adult created a love of the game for several of his players. How playing catch with his sons can be a form of therapy when he goes home. He talked about playing catch like I talk about playing catch, how it is a whole-body experience connecting two people like little else in sports.

And then he gave Kaylea and me each a marble.

"I'm convinced baseball is the best sport for life lessons. It teaches perseverance and humility. Ultimately, you're not in control, and you have to learn to surrender the outcome, to surrender the judgment. When I played at Crowder, when I had a bad game, the only ones who knew were my teammates. Now social media sends the message out practically everywhere. You just gotta outlast the other guy. Gotta have grit and simply outlast them."

I keep my marble right next to the baseball Sophie gave me for Christmas.

⚾ ⚾ ⚾

Nathan Rueckert's five-foot-wide map of leather and seams made its glorious debut just outside the main entrance of the National Baseball Hall of Fame in the spring of 2017 at the Cooperstown Symposium on Baseball and American Culture. I pulled up and parked my rental car and ran to see the map while dark skies threatened. Nathan and I posed for an iconic picture and quickly moved the map indoors to a safe and dry location.

Major League Baseball and Minor League Baseball and Independent League Baseball should tour the map across the country in as many ballparks as possible, making a display featuring that state's story with highlights from neighboring states. Invite those people to throw first pitches or to be special guests of the team for a night. Let patrons take free selfies and post pictures and share their own stories of how baseball is more than just a game.

I walked into the hallowed baseball hall and was greeted by four statues, men who played the game and shaped our culture: Lou Gehrig, Jackie Robinson, Roberto Clemente, and Buck O'Neil. Their baseball stories of passion, perseverance, and generosity are epic chapters proving that the game is more than a game.

As part of the symposium's closing session, Nathan and I were able to tell stories from the map, from its conception to its completion after two years. I was permitted to share some of my baseball poetry.

The resolute cork—
history wrapped in a century of string
encased in two strips of cowhide
bound together by
108 red, hand-sewn double stitches
and ninth-inning dreams.
The greatest of games testing

character, heart,
developing dogged perseverance.
True success:
a team who plays for one another
and for pure, unadulterated love of
the game.
Each ball, a narrative universe.
The Hit. The Catch. The Strikeout.
Last game. Last at bat. Last out.
Champions!
Sacred stories preserved in the seams,
passed along from generation to generation.
Though divided politically,
racially, religiously,
brought together through baseball—
America at the seams.

When it published, autographed copies of the coffee-table book sold in the gift shop. One of my friends sent me pictures of her copy after she purchased it there. My childhood dream came true: I made it into the National Baseball Hall of Fame.

Like every single other baseball player, announcer, and writer who makes it into the sacred halls of Cooperstown, I didn't make it because of my own efforts and abilities; I made it as part of a team. The greatest baseball players, those whose heroics are told time and time again, generously acknowledge the contributions of their teammates, who supported and encouraged their efforts. Like life, baseball beautifully combines individual and team effort. And like anything thrown from a southpaw, dreams rarely come true in a linear fashion. Years of grinding and hoping and digging deep and finding the right teammates are necessary. Nathan Rueckert was the reason I made it to Cooperstown.

11

Wallingford

The true object of all human life is play. Earth
is a task garden; heaven is a playground.
—G. K. CHESTERTON

"WHY ARE YOU GOING TO WALLINGFORD?"

"Where is Wallingford?"

"You know, there's another good baseball field you should visit while you're in Iowa."

The population of Wallingford, Iowa, is less than two hundred people. Ryan Cellan texted me detailed directions to make sure I wouldn't get lost. I got lost anyway. I ended up pulling a U-turn in an empty parking lot in search of the right street. It takes serious skills to get lost in a town as small as Wallingford.

Ryan loves the Minnesota Twins like I love the Kansas City Royals. He has a tattoo of the team's logo on his calf and his list of favorite players is a mile long. Kent Hrbek. Kirby Puckett. Harmon Killebrew. Joe Mauer.

"I met Kyle Gibson at TwinsFest," Ryan said as we played on day #150.

I know the name Kyle Gibson for two reasons. I interviewed Kyle for the Minnesota story for *America at the Seams*. Using his platform as a major league pitcher, Kyle has found a way to share his faith and express hope through service to others, whether in Minnesota or working in a partnership in Haiti. Kyle was also the starting pitcher against the Royals the night before I played catch with Ryan. The Royals never seem to do well against Kyle Gibson.

True to form, Gibson left the game with a 1–0 lead after seven innings. After tying the game in the eighth on a walk, the Royals won in the bottom of the fourteenth on an Alcides Escobar walk-off home run. I fell asleep sometime in the tenth inning. Even so, Ryan greeted me decked out in all things Twins.

"Just because you had a bad day yesterday doesn't mean you're not going to have a good day today," he said, stressing the importance of baseball players' choosing what to remember. Much like the spiritual practice called the "daily examen," which is designed to help pray-ers discern God's presence over the course of a day, it's wise to take a moment to reflect on the highs and the lows to see what can be learned about life and faith in those moments.

Ryan knows all about bad days.

Near the end of January 2013, he learned he had testicular cancer.

"After a shower one day, I noticed a lump that was painful. My wife told me to get it looked at, but I decided to wait. Not too long after that, I was in excruciating pain no matter what I did—sit, stand, whatever. My boss drove me to the emergency room, and I had surgery the next day. The following Monday, I had routine scans. I even went to the Mayo Clinic to make sure it was isolated and to explore next options. Visiting the cancer unit at the Mayo Clinic . . ."

Ryan took a deep breath. The doctors at the Mayo Clinic are some of the best in the world. Patients who go to the Mayo Clinic often go out of desperation.

"Being at the Mayo Clinic puts things in perspective. It makes you feel very fortunate. They caught the cancer early, so I didn't have to do any radiation or chemotherapy. I still have regular CAT scans and blood work and chest X-rays."

In December, Ryan had his annual blood work and received a call the following day that all tumor markers were normal.

"It's almost been six years now. I've had tons of CAT scans, X-rays, and blood work done. The worst part is waiting to get that call back. The minutes seem like years. Every time I go to the scans, every time I post updates, I say it: If anyone has questions or concerns regarding testicular cancer, don't hesitate to reach out. I'm more than willing to help out in any way I can."

A couple of months after receiving his diagnosis, Ryan and his family moved to Wallingford, Iowa, into a house that used to be the schoolhouse during the 1940s. The epitome of country living. Behind the former schoolhouse was a large field for crops—field corn in the odd years, beans in the even years. Next to the crop field, only eighty-eight steps from his back door to the first-base dugout, was an overgrown baseball field. There was a time when this field had lights and a press box, when multiple games were scheduled each week, when the town came out to support and cheer whoever was playing. I wondered how many Moonlight Grahams played ball on this field.

November 2013 was an election year in Wallingford, and Ryan decided to run for city council. He won. The next month, very early on Christmas morning, his second daughter was born—the gift of new life after what had to have felt like a death sentence at the beginning of that year.

As a newly elected member of city council, Ryan learned that the citizens of Wallingford wanted to turn the old baseball field into a dog park. Out of a pure and simple love for the game of baseball, Ryan took it upon himself to restore the baseball field.

Using an old chain-link fence, he started dragging the infield, trying to get rid of stubborn and strong weeds. A friend donated high-powered weed killer to the cause, which knocked out a majority of the weeds within a few days. He brought in three loads of proper material to replace the old pea-gravel infield. And the neighbors were support-ive. By the time I showed up to the Wallingford Ballfield, there were sponsor banners on the center-field fence that covered some of the ongoing costs of maintenance.

"There used to be a fastpitch softball team that played here. They were called the Wallingford Cruddies, so I'd love to officially name it Cruddy Field or something like that."

That name lends itself to marvelous T-shirt and marketing opportunities.

Ryan has since acquired proper maintenance equipment and con-tinues to improve the field. Six teams practiced and played on it in 2018, which is incredible considering it was overgrown and ignored just a couple of seasons ago. It hosted a women's softball tournament and a slowpitch league. He dreams of improving the fencing and add-ing permanent bathroom and concessions areas.

The drive to Ryan's field from Sioux Falls, South Dakota, was quiet and flat, and I needed to stretch a little bit before we could play catch. We started out on the infield and I made a few bad throws working the knots and kinks out of my back and shoulders. Ryan is helping coach a Little League team for the first time and sympathized with my soreness. Kaylea and Sophie grabbed gloves and spread out along the third-base line while Jamie unpacked a picnic lunch for us, complete with Dr Peppers courtesy of the Baseball Seams Company.

Once we had warmed up with thirty or forty throws, I moved to right field, and the left-handed-hitting Ryan hit me fly balls to chase down. The recent rains made the grass a little longer than the grass at the Storm Chasers' Werner Park (where I had been only two days before), but the hops were true and the overcast sky was perfect for tracking line drives and high pop-ups.

"My dream is for people to come here and have fun," Ryan said.

I was in heaven in Iowa.

⊘ ⊘ ⊘

Ninety-nine days later (day #249), I met Austin Kendrick, another survivor of testicular cancer.

Before I perfected my benchwarming skills at Kickapoo High School, during the summer between junior high and high school, I practiced my benchwarming skills at Parkview High School, playing on the school's summer American Legion team. I was so small, my green-striped jersey tucked into my tall socks. Occasionally I pitched or played middle infield or corner outfield, but mostly I cheered and clapped and made sure no foul balls were lost. Benchwarmers are important, too.

Austin is a Parkview graduate and now coaches basketball and baseball at the school. He also teaches physical education and leadership classes at the dragonless home of the Vikings. But before he coached, Austin chased his own baseball dreams.

"I signed a scholarship to play ball at Fort Scott," he said.

Two weeks after he graduated high school, however, Austin felt a small lump on one of his testicles during a routine self-check. As soon as he said this, I remembered Ryan's story.

"It was just a small lump, really. But I knew it was cancer immediately."

Once he detected the lump, life moved quickly. He visited the doctor on Monday and underwent a CAT scan on Tuesday. Wednesday was the day of the bad tidings of the official diagnosis, and Austin was on the surgery table on Saturday. Understandably, Fort Scott dropped his baseball scholarship. Austin decided to stay in Springfield and enrolled at Ozarks Technical Community College to start working on his general electives. On the first day of class, he got the results of the biopsy: eight weeks of chemotherapy were necessary.

And that was the end of Austin's professional baseball career.

Austin walked me over to the same baseball field where, thirty years prior, I'd spent a summer fielding grounders and chasing flies. The field had since received a facelift with the installation of artificial turf on the infield, making it possible for it to be both a softball field and a baseball field. I noticed Austin's first baseman's mitt, and after quickly warming up, he threw me grounders all over the middle infield. Each one a perfect hop, even if the shredded tires slowed the pace. I gave Austin several chances to practice scooping low throws.

While we played catch, Austin and I talked about the new, competitive wood-bat league, the Grip 'N' Rip Baseball League at U.S. Baseball Park in Ozark, Missouri. Austin spends Sundays in August and September in Ozark, where he coaches and plays for the A&L Electric Shockers.

"I love Grip 'N' Rip," Austin said. "It's my second chance to keep playing this game I love."

I went out the week before tryouts and shagged flies and caught during infield practice. I laughed when Justin Skinner, my catch partner on day #217, showed me his shoes—the turf was so hot it had melted the bottoms. I strongly considered trying out the following week, knowing that being on a team would help me find more catch partners during the dog days of the project. I ended up deciding against it, keeping my weekends open in case the Royals called.

There's always next year.[1]

---

1 And there was next year. I tried out for the Grip 'N' Rip League in 2019 and made the cut, playing for the CY Sports Cyclones. I was coached by two catch partners: Scott Nasby (day #344) and Ryan Wolfe (day #100).

⚾ ⚾ ⚾

Meeting Ryan and eating lunch at his field in Iowa was a breath of fresh air for my family as we traversed the state. Chasing down fly balls and playing catch, like Shoeless Joe's first appearance in *Field of Dreams,* filled me with wonder and optimism for the journey ahead. Ryan's story of healing and hope was a reminder to fully live the gift of each day. I was already dreaming of ways to get back to Wallingford to play again.

Throughout the year, I played catch with several people who played in the Grip 'N' Rip League and heard their stories of how much fun they had getting back on the field, too.

As an adult, creating time for fun takes effort. It does not necessarily require a trip to the northwest corner of Iowa, but I know that Ryan would gladly welcome anyone to Cruddy Field. It should not take the gravity of a cancer diagnosis to open our eyes to the importance of truly living the life we've been given. And the dogs in Wallingford are having fun, too. Wallingford built a dog park where the tennis courts used to be.

12

Iron Boy Bigby

Play is really the work of childhood.
—*Mister Rogers*

THE CATCH-PLAYING YEAR GREW INTO A PROJECT OF THE HEART.
Each day, I gave all of my attention to my catch-playing partners,
learning their stories while delighting in shared time tossing a ball. In
the early days and weeks, I was concerned I would burn out halfway
through the year or never want to play catch again if I actually suc-
ceeded in completing every day. Neither one could be farther from the
truth. As the year progressed, I grew more passionate about playing
catch, about discovering fun each and every day. Throughout the year,
I felt as if I was discovering the real me, the me God whispered into
creation, with each and every game of catch. Play is that sacred space
where we can best join in with the divine laughter and delight in who
we were made to be. No wonder we lose track of time playing: we are
dancing with one foot in eternity.

And games with the youngest catch partners were always an
adventure filled with whimsy and wonder.

Bigby is my godson. The only godparent I knew about growing up was the fairy godmother in Cinderella, but that doesn't help much, because it is serious work for me to turn a pumpkin into a mere jack-o'-lantern, much less a stagecoach for a princess. There is also the movie *The Godfather*, a story about life in a mafia family and a horse's head on a pillow, but I still haven't seen it.

I do not think I'm a very good godparent. Because of the distance between us, it has been almost three years since I last saw Bigby. Thankfully, it took about five seconds for him to warm up to me and the rest of my family when I visited him to play catch. The fearless, brown-eyed daredevil with the straight brown hair greeted me with a cheeky grin. "We are going to play baseball, right?" This is now my favorite greeting.

Just after he was born, it was discovered Bigby had tetralogy of Fallot, the same condition as that of comedian Jimmy Kimmel's son, with a couple of other little loopholes thrown in.

"If I had been born with Bigby's heart, I wouldn't have made it. We just didn't have the technology or know-how back then," Bigby's dad, Tim, said.

After Bigby's brothers left for field day at school, we celebrated Bigby's fourth birthday—a few weeks early—with gifts of Star Wars toys and a soft baseball. Both families then headed to the park to play catch (day #151). We found a great grassy location behind the Ferris wheel of the minor league Quad Cities River Bandits, right next to the mighty Mississippi River in Davenport, Iowa.

Tim and I started playing catch first, demonstrating how the glove is used for catching and the bare hand is used for throwing. Bigby quickly caught on and we worked into a rhythm. I'd throw the newly gifted birthday ball to Bigby. He'd throw it to Sophie. She'd throw it back to me. He then switched to a baseball Sophie had drawn on a couple of years ago. She'd decorated a baseball as a gift for a previous Christmas, creatively illustrating his name along with other drawings on it.

When playing catch with young kids or with catch-playing rookies, the important thing is not proper mechanics or grip or even stepping first with the foot opposite of the throwing arm. The important part is the fun. Keeping it fun engages both the imagination and the heart. Finding fun and sharing it with others is a needed superpower in today's stressed-out, play-deprived culture.

⚾ ⚾ ⚾

I think Bigby's story might be best told as a comic or a cartoon, with Sophie's help on the illustrations.

In June 2014, Bigby was born with a broken heart. There was a hole where there shouldn't be a hole, there were parts missing, and there were parts which seemed to be put in backward.

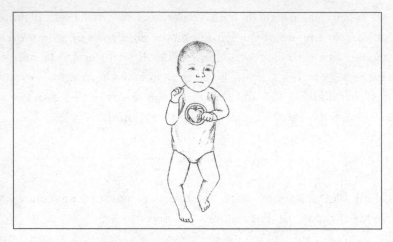

Six days later, Bigby had his first heart surgery. And that was the day Iron Boy Bigby was born.

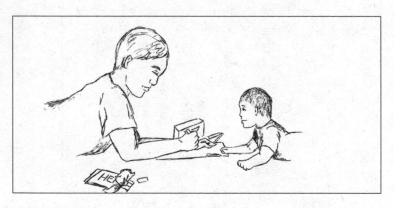

Iron Boy Bigby went home for the first time three weeks after his first surgery. His big brothers taught him about the important things in life: cartoons, crayons, and chocolate. Iron Boy was a little too small to understand everything they were saying, so he just smiled. Smiling is a grossly underrated superpower.

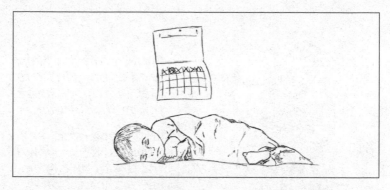

Six months later, Iron Boy Bigby had his second heart surgery. Doctors expected Bigby to spend weeks in the hospital recovering from the surgery. But superheroes often have special healing powers. Iron Boy Bigby went home four days later.

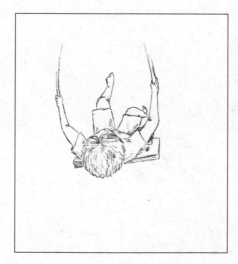

For three years, Iron Boy Bigby grew and did what boys do. He wrestled and played with his brothers. He watched cartoons and ate crayons and colored his face in with chocolate. He ran and jumped and made new friends at the playground.

One day Iron Boy Bigby tried to run a little too fast. He tripped and fell on the sidewalk.

He scraped knees and elbows and had a knot the size of an egg on his forehead. Such is the life of a growing superhero.

As he neared three years old, Bigby's heart couldn't keep up. He tired quite easily and took lots of naps. Doctors knew it was time for another surgery.

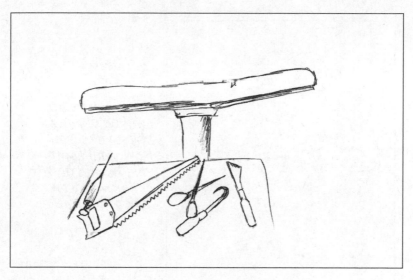

His parents tried to prepare him for the surgery, explaining how the doctors would have to cut open his chest to work on his heart. At first, Iron Boy didn't like the thought. He imagined big and scary things.

When his parents explained that this surgery would help him to run faster, to play longer, to better rid the world of evil, Iron Boy Bigby started to smile.

"I will run, run, run, fast, fast, fast!" he said with a gigantic grin.

"When I grow up, I will be big and strong like Iron Man. I will fight villains and go visit children in Iron Man's hospital."

Three days after his third heart surgery, Iron Boy Bigby was dancing in the hospital, bringing smiles to everyone around him. Superheroes are all about hope.

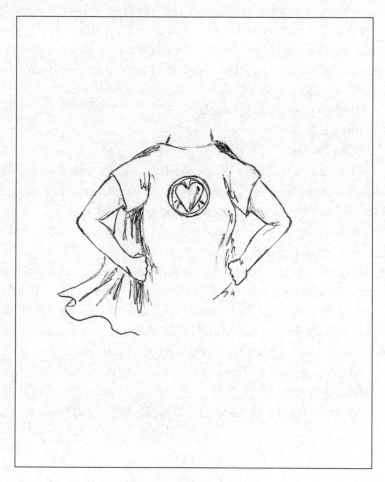

And superheroes require a special heart.

⚾ ⚾ ⚾

Right before we played catch, with the Mississippi River rushing by and the scenic carnival rides of the minor league ballpark as a perfect background, I tried to get a picture of Bigby on my phone, a personal reminder of our time together. He spotted me and my feeble efforts to capture anything other than a blur of legs and body parts.

"This is your phone?" he asked.

I nodded.

"Can I see it?"

I handed it to him and he opened and closed it several times. The distinctive clapping of a flip phone is simple entertainment for all ages. I scrolled to where his pictures were and he giggled.

"I like your phone," he commented before taking off in another blurry, fast-fast-fast run.

It's just a flip phone. The same kind Captain America used to connect with Iron Man in *Avengers: Infinity War*. And just like Captain America told Iron Man at the end of *Captain America: Civil War*, in my heart, I made a commitment to Bigby: "So no matter what, I promise you, if you need us, if you need me, I'll be there."

After catch, we posed for pictures, exchanged hugs and high fives, and loaded up the van.

My heart filled with hope for the stories Bigby will live.

13

A League of Their Own

Baseball is what gets inside you. It's what
lights you up, you can't deny that.
—JIMMY DUGAN, A LEAGUE OF THEIR OWN

THE SWELTERING HEAT FOLLOWED THE BRYAN FAMILY *MILLENNIUM Falcon* across Iowa and into Illinois. Despite the heat, we pressed on with our catch-playing Tour of Hope. Watching the speedometer consistently track above the speed limit, I was beside-myself excited to meet Mary and Perry. The *Falcon* was flying across the Iowa and Illinois interstates.

Baseball is a multigenerational sport. Veteran players pass along tricks of the trade to the rookies as well as putting them through their paces with various pranks. Stealing all the clothes from their lockers and replacing them with costumes, then returning the clothes the next day along with new suits and wallets full of cash. That's one of the nicer pranks. Players from decades past fill the stands sharing their stories with next-generation dreamers. Young players are encouraged and expected to trust the wisdom and insight of those who have been in their shoes. Playing catch turned out to be an epic activity for learning about life in the past.

My family accompanied me to Beyer Stadium, the home of the Rockford Peaches, and read the historic plaques while waiting for Mary Moore and Perry Barber to arrive. Work crews were finishing up preparations for the game celebrating the 75th anniversary of the creation of the All-American Girls Professional Baseball League, mowing and trimming the grass and making certain everything was in top-notch shape to honor the courageous women who played ball.

Mary Moore played second base for the Springfield Sallies and led the team in several offensive categories in 1950—hits, total bases, home runs, runs scored, and RBIs. After sustaining an injury to her throwing hand while at work in the off-season, she returned to form in 1952 only to sprain her ankle and end her career sliding into second.

"It would have been better if I broke it," Mary said.

I limped through half of each of 2015 and 2016 thanks to a broken ankle. It had to be surgically reconstructed, and now I have the utmost empathy for anyone who injures their ankle.

Perry Barber has been umpiring games since 1981 and works more than 150 games annually. A former *Jeopardy!* champion and a former singer-songwriter who once opened a concert for Bruce Springsteen, Perry is one of only a handful of professional female umpires. She helped me connect with Mary.

The first games of the All-American Girls Professional Baseball League were played on May 30, 1943, with the South Bend Blue Sox facing the Rockford Peaches at Beyer Stadium and the Kenosha Comets playing the Racine Belles at Horlick Field. The Racine Belles were the first league champions.

When I visited the National Baseball Hall of Fame, I was fascinated by the AAGPBL exhibition. On display were original uniforms, hats, and gloves of the league that inspired the movie *A League of Their Own*. I loved reading the story of speedster Sophie Kurys, who set the single-season stolen-base record, and I paid tribute to her in my Cooperstown poem.

I shook Buck's bronzed hand
courageous, compassionate
ambassador of the game
sweetly singing
the greatest thing in
all my life
is loving you

tipped my hat to
Gehrig, Robinson, Clemente
gentlemen giants
lucky men
impacting other lives
giving all they had to give

laughed with
Abbott and Costello
larger than life ageless Satchel
and smallest ever Gaedel

silently stood before Quiz
a heart of hope delivered
through flaws

thanked Aaron and Ruth
just keep swinging
through strikeout fears

remembered Ryan and Brett
coveted autographs
who quit playing
before we played catch

learned from
speedy Sophie Kurys
baseball is everyone's game.

"She's from Michigan," Mary said. "They used to call her the Flint Flash. Once she got on first base, she'd be on third base two pitches later."

Two days after the 75th anniversary of the first AAGPBL games, I was in Rockford, Illinois, at Beyer Stadium. Mary and Perry and several other ballplayers were in Rockford launching a $7 million campaign to build the International Women's Baseball Center and Museum.

"The center and museum will be right across the street from the field," Perry said. "It's really a dream come true. Not only will it honor the history of AAGBPL and the ladies who played in the league, but it will honor the history that preceded them and makes it possible for girls to continue participating in the game. And there will also be good green space for umpiring training!"

At eighty-six, Mary was one of my oldest catch partners (day #152). She and I played catch just outside the newly repainted third-base dugout, and Perry filmed a few moments, which made me somewhat nervous. Then again, I always get nervous when I play catch with a professional ballplayer. I loved the old Wilson glove Mary was using. She laughed when I showed her the even older Wilson I was going to use.

I asked her about her best day on the field.

"The triple play we turned against Chicago. They were all tag plays, no force outs, no fly balls. They had runners on first and second and the gal hit a ball to left field. The runner on second tried to score, but she got caught in a rundown between home and third and was tagged out. The runner on first was headed to third but stopped and ran back toward second. The hitter had rounded first and was also headed to second. I was standing on second, and they threw me the ball and I tagged them both to end the inning."

Kaylea and Sophie joined in the game as Mary continued to teach us and share her stories.

"Baseball gets in your head, in your mind, in your body. You get to go outside in the fresh air and meet new people. It teaches you discipline and respect. This game teaches you all kinds of life lessons," Mary said. "You don't have to like people to play ball with them. We learned to cooperate, to be disciplined, to treat others with respect. The whole world was different. Money didn't mean anything in particular. We played for the love of the game."

Perry added, "I love the energy of the game. The way it makes people think as well as react. The way it engages both mind and soul. There's so much to love about it. It's not all the pomp and spectacle of the major leagues. It's something as simple as a game of catch and talking about stuff that matters and making friends."

Mary not only played in the league, she also appeared in the 1992 movie directed by Penny Marshall and starring Tom Hanks, Geena Davis, and Lori Petty.[1]

"I was the one that slid into home," Mary said. "If you watch through the credits, you'll see me. I was playing left field in that game. You can also spot me walking into the Hall of Fame and stopping to take a picture. I was a designated Canadian for the team cheers."

We were playing catch at the field where Mary's career with the

---

1   In the movie, she plays her older self walking into the Hall of Fame and taking a picture. She's also seen singing as a Canadian. At the end of the movie, during the credits, the former players play an actual game and she slides into home.

AAGPBL ended. But Mary expressed no regrets. She seemed thrilled to play the game, to know that she was good enough to be a professional ballplayer.

⊘ ⊘ ⊘

It is hard to admit that I am not good enough, that my sheer passion for the game doesn't translate to on-field ability and seven-figure success. That's the fear anyone faces when they try out for a team, when they take a test, when they apply for a job—that they will be judged and deemed not good enough. Life is filled with "not good enough" moments.

Unrequited affection.

Seeking a promotion.

Implementing new diet and exercise routines.

"Baseball is life," Mary said. "Anything you learn from or about baseball can be applied to your daily life, to any relationship you have. When I observe ballplayers, those who succeed are the ones who absorb the lessons in front of them instead of getting angry. Anger prevents them from being successful. That's the difference. It's not about talent, really, but harnessing the energy and not allowing their emotions to master them. They know how to make their emotions work for them, so the result is what they want."

How are you supposed to reply to being told you're not good enough?

You don't throw hard enough to play varsity.

Your grades aren't good enough for the scholarship.

There are better applicants for the position.

Those moments I have sat with my not-good-enoughness are initially met with a melancholic disappointment. I console myself with the simple, honest truth: *At least I tried. I held nothing back and gave it my best effort. I poured my heart into it and have no regrets.* Those words, often accompanied by a Dr Pepper and a donut, are usually sufficient encouragement to short-circuit my pity party and keep me dreaming.

How are you supposed to reply when you know you're good enough, but life prevents you from getting a chance?

⚾ ⚾ ⚾

Ninety-eight days after Mary and I played catch in Rockford, on a dark and stormy day, we played catch a second time in Kansas City at the Negro Leagues Baseball Museum (day #250). Tropical Storm Gordon was a faithful travel companion all the way from Springfield to Kansas City. Strong winds and steady rain were regularly interrupted by the rhythmic clicking of the windshield wipers. I stopped at the halfway point to stretch my shoulders and relax my cramping fingers.

Shortly after getting back in the van and resuming the northbound driving portion of the trip, I spotted a bald eagle sitting stalwart in a tree, seemingly daring the winds to move him from his post. Images of that eagle occupied my mind as I pressed on to downtown KC. The skyline I'm used to seeing disappeared into the intimidating clouds. At least the Royals were on the road, too.

The All-American Girls Professional Baseball League was hosting its 75th reunion in Kansas City. Mary and Perry were in my neck of the woods. On 18th and Vine, in the jazz district, is the Negro Leagues Baseball Museum, full of stories of those who were good enough. Unfortunately, the vast majority were never given the opportunity to play in the major leagues simply because of the skin God painted on them.

Dressed in a stunning blue-checked suit, two-tone wingtips, and matching fedora, NLBM president Bob Kendrick greeted me with a hug and a handshake moments after I walked in the doors.

"Great to see you!"

"Gonna be a fun group to tour the museum with," I replied.

I've played catch with Bob on multiple occasions, delighting in his stories and the truths he shares of the men and women who played baseball, proving they were more than good enough to play with and against their white counterparts.

I played catch with Bob in February (day #34). On the Field of Legends, I stood next to the Satchel Paige statue while Bob positioned himself near Josh Gibson. The stories he tells and the lessons he shares on how baseball provided a way to fight racism, hate, and violence need to be broadcast nationally.

"I delight in telling these stories because I'm contributing to a legacy that is bigger than just me," Bob said between tosses. He made me smile when he connected what I was doing to Buck O'Neil, one of the game's best ambassadors. "The ideology of playing catch emphasizes everything Buck loves about the game."

Mary and Perry entered the atrium between the NLBM and the Jazz Museum. Perry introduced me to several other players as Bob greeted the ballplayers and their families. The storytelling commenced with tales of Buck O'Neil, Cool Papa Bell, and Josh Gibson. Before the walking tour started, Bob concluded with the following Satchel Paige legend: The Bourbon Story.

"Bill Veeck used to own a Triple-A minor-league team, the Miami Marlins, and Whitey Herzog and Satchel Paige were teammates. Veeck, ever the creative promotional genius, used a hole in the center-field fence as a gimmick, and offered a substantial sum for any hitter who could hit the ball through the hole on the fly.

"Before one game, Whitey went out to center field to see if he could throw a ball through the hole. He sized it to make sure a ball would fit, but had no success throwing a ball through it despite hundreds and hundreds of attempts. Whitey started talking to Satchel, who was known for his pinpoint control. It's said that Satchel used to warm up throwing pitches over gum wrappers.

"'Satch, you see that hole out there in center field?'

"And Satchel called Whitey 'Wild Child.'

"'Yes, Wild Child.'

"'I'll bet you a bottle of bourbon you can't throw the ball through that hole.'

"'Wild Child, does the ball in fact fit through the hole?'

"'Satch, it sure does.'

"'Then you have a bet.'

"The next day, they went out to center field and paced off sixty feet, six inches. Satchel stood and looked over his arm, like sighting a rifle. On the first throw, the ball circled the hole, like lipping out a putt, but it didn't go through. Whitey couldn't believe how close Satchel had come. And then Satchel threw the ball through the hole on the second attempt.

"Satchel walked back to the dugout one bottle of Old Forester bourbon richer."

The atrium echoed with laughter and applause.

Touring the Negro Leagues Baseball Museum with the women of the AAGPBL while listening to Bob's stories was a glimpse into everything good about life. Bob shared the stories behind the new *Beauty of the Game* exhibit featuring the ladies who played in the Negro Leagues—Connie Morgan, Toni Stone, and Mamie Johnson. I saw many affirming nods of understanding; these stories were their stories, too.

Once the tour concluded, I ran into Mary on the Field of Legends.

"Are you interested in another game of catch?"

"Absolutely!"

We positioned ourselves between Satchel Paige and Josh Gibson and started throwing. In short order, Terry joined us.

Terry McKinley Uselmann is an outfielder from Chicago and a Notre Dame fan. She played one season with the Muskegon Lassies and told a hilarious story about being fined two dollars in her first game.

"I bunted in my first at bat and promptly stole second base. When I got back to the dugout, I was fined the first dollar for bunting, then another dollar for stealing. Up until that point, the coach hadn't given me any signs or said anything to me!"

As the three of us played catch surrounded by bronze statues and living legends, several people took pictures and recorded videos, but no one else joined in. A couple of players commented how much they enjoyed watching us and passed around my old Wilson glove.

⚾ ⚾ ⚾

How are you supposed to reply when you know you're good enough, but life prevents you from getting a chance?

No girls are allowed to play in this league.

Your skin is the wrong color.

You don't have the right education.

"The story of these men, these ballplayers, is a story not about the adversity but about everything they did to overcome that adversity," Bob said. "These men simply dreamed of playing a game, and they ended up making history. Their passion, their dedication, their courage not only changed the game, but it changed the country."

How are you supposed to reply when you know you're good enough, but life prevents you from getting a chance?

Keep playing anyway.

Keep dreaming anyway.

Dare to laugh and have fun anyway.

And whatever you do, don't give up, because people and circumstances can change.

Tom Hanks's character Jimmy Dugan said it best in *A League of Their Own*: "It's supposed to be hard! If it wasn't hard, everyone would do it. The hard . . . is what makes it great!"

14

Together

All good stories deserve a little embellishment.
—GANDALF, THE HOBBIT

CHICAGO IS THE THIRD LARGEST CITY IN THE UNITED STATES WITH a city population around 2.7 million and a metro-area population of 9.5 million—roughly seventeen times the size of Springfield. After visiting with Mary and Perry, I successfully drove the Bryan Family *Millennium Falcon* through the heart of Chicago on the way to our hotel. I navigated the Magnificent Mile and passed Millennium Park. I survived swerving buses and daring pedestrians and eventually found parking near Navy Pier.

The Windy City lived up to its nickname. After enduring eight days of triple-digit heat, we found biting Lake Michigan winds cutting our photo-taking, memory-making, anchor-visiting time short. I did not pack the right clothes for that kind of weather. The winds were so strong the famous Ferris wheel was closed. I lasted mere minutes posing for a family picture by the anchor of the USS *Chicago* as wind whipped the flags into a frenzy and tried multiple times to send my hat into Lake Michigan. We sought shelter indoors to warm up, and then walked to the nearby beach and kicked the sand. The winds subsided long enough for the Ferris wheel to open, and we were able to take in the sights of skyscrapers while turning in circles.

And then I forgot where I parked the van.

The key fob that is supposed to help in such situations was useless. I'd tried to replace the battery before the trip only to discover the interior was corroded. I am fine with manually locking and unlocking the vehicle; I just didn't think ahead to a where-the-heck-did-I-park scenario. It took only thirty minutes of touring the parking garage to find the *Falcon,* at which point I resolved never to drive in Chicago again.

Thanks to remarkable Metra drivers and bus drivers and a little luck, I didn't have to attempt navigating through the throngs of people the next morning. I wore my "Wanna Play Catch?" T-shirt and a young man nudged me. "I'd love to play catch!"

I had only one glove in my backpack. I'd trusted that my catch partners for day #153, Shane and Shaun Lamie, would bring theirs.

"If you've got a glove, I've got mine," I said to the young man.

"Maybe next time," he said, smiling.

My family and I caught an express train and walked up to Millennium Park almost exactly when we'd planned to arrive. We took in some sightseeing along Madison Street, passing by the columns of the Lyric Opera and craning our necks to see the tops of buildings as we walked among the hurried morning-commute crowd.

Since the park was hosting the Chicago Gospel Music Festival— fantastic background music for a game of catch—we had to pass through security before we were admitted entrance. Shane and Shaun were waiting for me by *Cloud Gate,* the mirrored statue better known as *The Bean.* The identical twin brothers introduced themselves: Shane in the Chicago Cubs hat, Shaun in the Cincinnati Reds hat. A few years younger than me, they wore matching blue, sleeveless softball jerseys, looking like they could step onto the field and play a doubleheader without breaking a sweat. Before my family and I arrived, the brothers had visited with a security guard and received permission to use the grass field at the back of the Jay Pritzker Pavilion, the open-air amphitheater, to play catch. There was no shortage of obstacles, people and hanging speakers being the primary two to avoid. We found great space at the back of the park, with wonderful throwing lanes. There were only a couple of occasions we had to wait while unobservant patrons walked in the middle of our game of catch.

I overheard multiple onlookers commenting on the "baseball players," wondering who we were and what we were doing. Shane threw forkballs that danced like knuckleballs, and Shaun and I played long toss, spread out as far as the Navy Pier Ferris wheel is tall, successfully avoiding beams and speakers with each throw. In Chicago, I felt I was most truly me; I was at my best.

The catch-playing tour of the Midwest was not a prototypical hero's journey. The trials and tribulations were minor: record-setting heat and traveling long distances. No sicknesses or automotive problems or injuries to my arm. No evil was conquered and no wrongs were set right, so I wasn't really a hero at all. It was closer to a Griswold family adventure, except everything went as planned. Even so, I discovered the sheer joy that is often seen at the end of favorite books and movies.

I am at my best spending significant time with my family, exploring new places, making new memories, getting lost and laughing about it.

I am at my best connecting to new friends through the game of baseball, uncovering the good and hopeful in people.

I am at my best creating space for fun to celebrate life with others, stepping away from the screens and constant bombardment of stress and pressure and online vitriol between strangers over every single topic.

I am at my best telling and writing stories.

I didn't want the trip to end. I didn't want to go back home and return to normal life, but this was the next-to-the-last day of the Tour of Hope. The next day, we would journey home. From sunrise to sunset, I made the most of every waking moment with my family.

Jamie and I had talked about the possibility of heading south so I could connect with Aaron Unthank in Jacksonville, Florida. Aaron is a musician with a silky-smooth tenor voice who loves baseball as much as I do, even if he cheers for the other Missouri MLB team. From the very beginning of the catch-playing year, Aaron cheered and encouraged me on through every adventure, commenting on almost every blog post.

When Jamie and I first explored potential itineraries, the trip south seemed too far. The van needed some minor work and I didn't have a clue who I would find to play catch with along the way. A second catch-playing trip would exhaust our savings. There were far more questions than answers.

But the Tour of Hope confirmed that heading south was worth the risk. On the last night of the tour, after devouring deep-dish pizza and reliving our day of twenty thousand steps in Chicago, we committed to taking a second catch-playing trip. While resting in the hotel, I started sending out emails explaining who I was and what I was doing.

Expect rejection; rejoice in the exception.

⚾ ⚾ ⚾

When Shaun Lamie first emailed me back in January, I laughed at the prospect of heading to Chicago to play catch. Both brothers saw my story on MLB.com. Shaun tracked down my blog and reached out to me without a second thought. The brothers worked at the same corporation, and they had played catch together over lunch breaks for years.

"Baseball is a universal language," Shaun said when we finally met in person in Chicago. "You can pick up a glove and a ball with a complete stranger, not even able to speak to each other, and still be able to start a game of catch." We were living proof of his statement.

Shane added, "And anyone really can play. It doesn't matter what size you are—from José Altuve to Aaron Judge."

I laughed because we had both seen the same picture portraying the differences between the two players. Altuve stands five foot six. Judge is *thirteen* inches taller.

I invited the brothers to come to Springfield for our second game of catch. About one hundred days later, they took me up on the offer—Shaun on day #258 and Shane on day #259.

Over the course of two days, I took Shaun and Shane on a catch-playing tour of the Queen City of the Ozarks, stopping at all the locations I had played catch as well as other notable sights: Bass Pro Shops, St. George's Donuts, Missouri State University, and Hammons Field. We finished with a trip to the best quarter-slot batting cages, followed by cashew chicken and Andy's Frozen Custard.

Three days before Christmas, Shaun and Shane sent me a letter.

Ethan,

I feel like this could almost be the start of a joke . . . "Three guys walk into a bar—a Royals fan, a Cubs fan, and a Bulls fan."

A year ago, Shane and I didn't even know you lived on this planet.

Then you wanted to play catch . . .

We reached out to you and first met you and your family next to *The Bean* in Chicago. I'm not sure if you knew what kind of day it was going to be, but for us it was a chance to be a part of something special.

We sat at the bench next to *The Bean,* talking and wondering what was going through your mind . . . what can it feel like to walk into a big city like Chicago to meet a couple of complete strangers for a game of catch?

We really hoped all the feelings or worries you had would disappear once we shook hands the first time.

It was truly a great experience!

Months went by and your story continued. We kept up with it every day and usually caught up with each other later in the day. "Did you see Ethan's post today?" We needed to do it again.

So we did. This time on your turf.

We got in the car and drove, seeing sights our eyes had never seen before and eating food we'd never tasted.

You welcomed us into your house and made us feel like a part of your family. Playing games, sharing stories, taking batting practice, and screaming on rollercoasters.

Words can't even explain how great it feels . . . baseball . . . a game of catch. Complete strangers a year ago and now as close to friends as states away can be.

We need to do it again!

Thank you Ethan, Jamie, Kaylea, and Sophie.

Shaun and Shane

Accompanying the letter was a Buck O'Neil autographed baseball, some autographed Royals baseball cards, and a new board game for my family.

All because we played catch.

Because I said yes to the inspired whispered invitation to play catch every day.

And because my family agreed to spend ten days on the road to see what happened.

⚾ ⚾ ⚾

The 365 days of 2018 turned into a year of making new friends, of reaching out and pushing boundaries, of handshakes and high fives. I learned that it is easy to grow comfortable in our routines, keeping communities small and safe and same and familiar. Extending playful hospitality by inviting strangers into the experiment turned out to be a serendipitous adventure of celebrating the beauty and brokenness found in the world.

The population of Springfield, Missouri, is 92 percent white, a fact which can be directly attributed to a horribly unjust lynching that took place on Good Friday in 1906. John Sellars is executive director of the History Museum on the Square, and I played catch with him on Good Friday and listened to his retelling of the horrific event (day #89).[1]

A woman from Fair Play, Missouri, hooked up with a traveling salesman. The two claimed they were assaulted and robbed, falsely accusing two young black men as assailants. In a series of acts driven by hate and fear of someone who looked different, three young men were lynched and burned in the middle of the square without a trial. A small plaque now remembers their deaths.

"It's still hard for me to talk about," John said. "Even 112 years later, such a gruesome, heinous act. It started to make national news on the East Coast and would have put Springfield on the map, but the earthquake in San Francisco on Easter [in 1906] changed all that. Understandably, immediately the African American population hid in sheer terror. They hid in houses and churches, and a steady exodus left Springfield, going to Tulsa or Kansas City or St. Louis. In a growing city that was progressive and thought to be welcoming, a city that once had a black population of 12 percent, it now dropped down below 1.

"It is important, imperative to remember stories like this. It explains how we got to where we are and, hopefully, serves as a cautionary tale of how people's fear and lack of tolerance can impact generations. What we need to do after hearing and reflecting on these

---

1   After significant remodeling, the History Museum on the Square was voted the #1 Best New Attraction by *USA Today* in 2019. Learn more about it here: http://historymuseum onthesquare.org/.

stories is not turn and walk away. What we need to do is put our arms around one another and commit to making the future brighter and better. Together."

Throughout the year, I tried my best to capture my catch partner's stories so I could remember, reflect, and learn. We tell stories to connect with other people and make new friends. We tell stories so we can face tomorrow's unknowns with courage. We tell stories to help us make sense of the world and discover hope in it. I delighted in each of my catch partners and relished every single story they told.

Just a few weeks before we played catch, Lester Ratcliff experienced some of that same ignorant, racist hatred—in 2018.

"I was just playing with my kids at the park when someone drove by and shouted the N word at us. I don't go around looking for racism, but it's there. There's a fine line between racism and ignorance, and education and relationships are the way forward."

On the day Major League Baseball celebrated Jackie Robinson Day, I played catch with Lester, a middle-school teacher and umpire (day #105). Lester knows the power of stories, relationships, and baseball.

"Jackie's legacy still teaches us today that we can tolerate people at their worst, whether or not we like them. Some of his teammates didn't want to play with him merely based on perception; they didn't know him at all. What he did on the field opened the doors for conversations—for hard, important conversations—and that leads to relationship, where you really get to know people. Those relationships create real change."

On January 1, 2018, I had a wonderful game of catch with each of my daughters. I didn't know that was the beginning of an adventure-filled year.

Because of a wonderful game of catch, I spent a year practicing skills necessary for success both on and off the field—cooperation, trust, and communication.

Because of a wonderful game of catch, I spent a year going places and discovering over and over again one of God's greatest gifts on the journey of life—friends, new and old.

And just like a wonderful game of catch, I hold on to hope for the future, because real, necessary, important change will happen as we choose to move forward together.

15
Raising Dreamers

Your life is an occasion. Rise to it.
—Mr. Magorium, Mr. Magorium's Wonder Emporium

I grew up playing catch with Dad. In the church parking lot across the street, the same parking lot where he taught me how to drive on ice, the same parking lot where I learned how to rollerskate and ride a ten-speed bike, our baseballs got blackened by the asphalt and occasionally lost in the bushes at the edge of the church's property. Dad regifted one of the "lost" baseballs to me one Christmas. We played catch in the back yard between the blue spruce and the southern white pine and the sweetgum and crimson king maple trees where a fastball high and tight put a hole in the middle of our storage shed. The shed and all the trees except the maple are gone, but I hope to keep the low-sixties fastball for a few more years. We played catch in the middle of the street, where we had to dodge neighbors' cars turning the corner on their drive home. From second grade through age sixteen, the nigh-electric pop of leather and the feeling of the seams beneath my fingertips provided the foundation for our relationship.

My on-field skills peaked as a benchwarmer for the junior varsity team of Kickapoo High School, but my love for the game has only increased in the decades since.

⚾ ⚾ ⚾

As my family and I traveled mile after mile in the Bryan Family *Millennium Falcon,* dented and dusty and donut-and-Dr-Pepper powered, we talked. We talked about the new friends we'd made and the plans for the next day and the scenery we saw or the lack thereof. The roaring falls and the golden cornfields and the windmill farms—"They are trying to cool everything off in this heat"—and the whitecapped waves of Lake Michigan. Jamie and I took pictures, and I made notes because so many of my catch-playing friends told me how they also grew up playing catch with their dads, how much they wished they could have one more game of catch with them.

As we crisscrossed Iowa, the *Field of Dreams* conversation between Ray Kinsella and Terence Mann played often in my brain: "He never made it as ballplayer, so he tried to get his son to make it for him. By the time I was ten, playing baseball got to be like eating vegetables or taking out the garbage, so when I was fourteen, I started to refuse. Can you believe that? An American boy refusing to have a catch with his father."

I am grateful the quote doesn't apply to me and Dad.

⚾ ⚾ ⚾

To echo Hagrid from the Harry Potter series, "Blood's important."

This beautifully quixotic catch-playing "quest" started because of a conversation with my daughters that lasted the first few days of the year. The memories made on the movie-inspired Catch 365 Tour of Hope were as precious, as valuable, as my backpack of gloves. From record-high triple-digit temperatures in Omaha to windy fifties in Chicago, we had a thoroughly midwestern adventure. We spent time with family and made new friends and saw wonders of both nature and human creativity. We tried our best to extend hope and kindness wherever we went and saw them reflected back to us time and time again by complete strangers.

From the pastry chef who gave me free macaroons. The purple ones were perfection.

From the animal trainers at the Lincoln Park Zoo who patiently answered all of Sophie's questions.

From the friends who provided us with beds and meals and hot showers.

From the children who laughed and played and welcomed us into their homes.

From the bus driver and passengers who helped us find our way through downtown Chicago.

From the porter who told us stories of his family's survival and recovery in Puerto Rico.

And, of course, from everyone we met through games of catch.

I could not have made it through this year without the help, encouragement, and participation of my family. The foundation for the year of playing catch was laid in the parking lot, in the back yard, and in the middle of the street with Dad.

⚾ ⚾ ⚾

There is a new baseball team in Chicago—the Chicago Dogs. They're part of the American Association of Independent Professional Baseball, playing teams like the Kansas City T-Bones, Sioux Falls Canaries, and Winnipeg Goldeyes. I had emailed and left messages for people in the front office in the weeks leading up to the trip, but never heard any replies. No response was standard fare for most professional teams I contacted. I figured they must get ridiculous requests all the time; they can't say yes to everyone. My backup plan was to play catch with my daughters in the parking lot in front of the new stadium.

We loaded up the van and started the journey home. Newly constructed Impact Field was thirty minutes down the road. Traffic was heavy as we neared O'Hare International Airport. A concert of some kind was scheduled directly across the street from the stadium, creating more traffic and some confusion with the parking attendants. We eventually parked the van next to a nondescript office building, walked up to the stadium, and started tossing a ball when one of the executives spotted us. He invited us to meet him at the players' entrance so we could play catch in center field before the teams started warming up (day #154).

The blue and red Chicago Dogs logo danced on the jumbotron underneath a cloudless, powder-blue sky. I walked carefully onto the freshly cut and rolled grass and soaked in the sun, permanently etching hat-tan lines onto my bald head, absorbing as much vitamin D into my system as possible before the long drive. Standing in center field, delighting in this brand-new stadium and celebrating this children's game, I was struck with a simple truth: I was the dad.

A cowboy at heart, my dad is a chemist-turned-veterinarian whose days on the diamond were limited to pitching in a church recreational softball league in the boot heel of Missouri. As a senior in high school, he paced the sidelines on the varsity football team as a late-game defensive replacement. Baseball wasn't his sport. Dad played catch in support of my dreams, to help me find my way in this world and make the most of my abilities.

The themes of fatherhood and the passage of time so evident in *Field of Dreams* were now playing out in real life. I was the dad in Kaylea's dream-chasing story, dreams centered around music. Playing the violin. Teaching music to others. Bringing hope and joy into the world through melodies and harmonies and Broadway productions and movie soundtracks.

I was the dad in Sophie's dream-chasing story, dreams centered around art. Creating visual masterpieces. Connecting people through an ever-growing variety of media. Bringing hope and joy into the world through paintings and sketches and stop-motion videos and cat training.

None of their dreams have anything to do with baseball. Maybe, just maybe, as I include them in the work of my dreams, they will learn firsthand lessons about chasing dreams with all of their hearts. Maybe they will catch a glimpse of the tenacity and perseverance necessary to do good work and refuse to give up in the face of whatever obstacles they encounter.

With every breath I breathe, I believe one of my most important responsibilities as a dad is to encourage and support my daughters as they learn to do the work of turning their dreams into realities. In the movie *Up in the Air*, George Clooney's character is brought in to fire J. K. Simmons' character. Understandably, Simmons is furious until Clooney asks, "How much did they first pay you to give up on your dreams?" As Walt Disney said, "All our dreams can come true, if we have the courage to pursue them."[1]

Raising dreamers begins with a modified definition of success.[2] Success is not measured by treasure or trophies; each of those invites a dragon to come into one's life. Success is simply the lifelong journey of growing in love for all people. Raising dreamers is rooted in love and expressed relationally.

---

1   Lewis Howes, "Twenty Lessons from Walt Disney on Entrepreneurship, Innovation, and Chasing Your Dreams," *Forbes*, July 17, 2012, https://www.forbes.com/sites/lewishowes /2012/07/17/20-business-quotes-and-lessons-from-walt-disney/#7b607ea84ba9, accessed February 2020.

2   I wrote more about raising dreamers in my essay "Raising Dreamers," in *Father Factor: American Christian Men on Fatherhood and Faith*, ed. R. Anderson Campbell, I Speak for Myself no. 5 (Ashland, OR: White Cloud Press), 2014.

Raising dreamers encourages taking risks and experiencing failure and rejection and then daring to risk again to create anew. Engaging the world invites criticism and rejection from others. Some will point and laugh. I know from experience how hard it is not to take the negative responses of others personally. Chase dreams anyway.

Between the Dreaming and the Coming True is the title of Robert Benson's first book and one of my favorites. It is also that sacred space where "Resistance" (thanks, Steven Pressfield) is fought and living with all of your heart makes a difference. Too many people shut themselves off after experiencing rejection and setback, refusing to trust anyone or try again. Like any journey worth taking, like any story worth reading, like any adventure worth living, life is full of highs and lows.

Do not give up.

⚾ ⚾ ⚾

I meant to buy a Chicago Dogs T-shirt for my trip souvenir but completely forgot. Since we were actually on the field, we never made it near any of the vendors. We walked back to the van and Kaylea and Sophie decided to watch *Mr. Magorium's Wonder Emporium*, a fantastic movie of whimsy that perfectly describes this year of playing catch.

Knowing how much I love their words, both Kaylea and Sophie wrote me letters for Christmas about the year. Like the baseball from the year before, part of Sophie's gift included her art, its creative packaging. She cut her letter into five sections, then glued them inside of an origami box which was sealed closed by two semicircular clasps decorated to look like a baseball.

Merry Christmas, Dad!
This year has been crazy. I'm amazed by your persistence and I love the adventures we've been on, and the friends as well as the

memories we've made.

I don't think I realized before this year how many people you can connect with and how many stories you can hear just by playing catch.

When this whole thing started, I was slightly doubtful about how you would get enough people to play catch with you, especially complete strangers. I didn't understand why anyone would really want to play catch.

Now I think I understand.

I think everyone just wants to play and have fun, to get outdoors and meet other people and to share their stories. For some people, people who haven't played catch in five, ten, twenty years, it brings back memories.

We've learned that play is good for us and it brings people together. I think people get so wrapped up with work, they forget that they still need and want to play. From ages two to ninety, we still want to have fun. And what better way to do that than to play catch?

The sealed-envelope packaging of Kaylea's letter with her fancy handscript was more standard fare.

Dad,

This year has definitely been crazy. I have learned so much!

1. Ask ridiculous questions! So many people would be too scared to put themselves out there or ask someone to do something with them. But by doing so, the answer is automatically no.

2. Learn about people. Listen with intention. I love hearing all the stories you've learned just through playing catch. Talking to people and being kind and genuine is so important. And by playing catch, you eliminated the distractions of technology that often interfere. Being present is so much more important. You've shown that to me time and time again, and I appreciate it.

3. Persevere. This has been a recurring theme in both of our

lives. For me, with school and violin and just pushing through when things aren't easy. For you, it meant still playing catch on rainy days and when you didn't feel like it (if that even happens) and especially when you couldn't find someone for a certain day. But you did it!

4. Play. I know you emphasized this this year, but it is so important to take a break and go back to being a kid. We all really are just kids at heart.

5. Have fun. This goes along with the importance of play, but sometimes we just need to not take ourselves so seriously. Enjoying what we're doing is so important and so is enjoying the people we're with.

Merry Christmas, Dad!

Kaylea

⚾ ⚾ ⚾

David Ogden is a professor emeritus at the University of Nebraska Omaha. In a discussion about the declining numbers of young athletes playing baseball, he wrote, "We are looking at a generation who didn't play catch with their dads."[3] Tears welled up in my eyes when I first read that. And from the National Fatherhood Initiative: "According to the US Census Bureau, 19.7 million children, more than 1 in 4, live without a father in the home."[4] Millions of kids are growing up

---

3   Marc Fisher, "Baseball Is Struggling to Hook Kids—and Risks Losing Fans to Other Sports," *Washington Post*, April 5, 2015, https://www.washingtonpost.com/sports/nationals/baseballs-trouble-with-the-youth-curve--and-what-that-means-for-the-game/2015/04/05/2da36dca-d7e8-11e4-8103-fa84725dbf9d_story.html; William Mattox, "Playing Catch with Pop," Heritage.org, July 20, 2017, https://www.heritage.org/2017-index-culture-and-opportunity/playing-catch-pop.

4   "The Proof Is In: Father Absence Harms Children," National Fatherhood Initiative, https://www.fatherhood.org/father-absence-statistic.

without fathers active in their lives, kids whose dads aren't present to teach them anything, much less how to play catch.

Reading and rereading and rereading Sophie's and Kaylea's letters, I am amazed and humbled by how much they've learned simply because we've spent time together, traversing states and traipsing on ball fields. And I am learning so much from them. They are teaching me to see the world in new ways, where music shapes minds and colors play in daily dawns and dusks. Their dreams are helping give shape to my dreams, where interdisciplinary play helps us be better people, giving me confidence to keep taking new risks.

After playing catch with Tim Flattery, aka Moonlight Graham (day #207), I was a guest on *The Moonlight Graham Show*.[5] In an in-home studio, surrounded by fascinating memorabilia from all sports, Tim ended the interview with the question, "What are you most proud of in life?"

"I'm most proud of the relationship I have with my daughters," I answered without a beat. "They are amazing, amazing young women."

In *Shoeless Joe*, the fictionalized J. D. Salinger says, "If I had my life to live over again, I'd take more chances. I'd want more passion in my life. Less fear and more passion, more risk. Even if you fail, you've still taken a risk."[6]

Jesus once told a story about risks and rewards, about the distribution of talents, about a man of nobility who entrusted his servants with money and gave them simple instructions: "Operate with this until I return" (Luke 19:11–27 MSG). Some of the servants did as they were told and reaped enormous rewards. One servant simply held on to the funds. "To tell you the truth, I was a little afraid. I know you have

---

5   "Ethan Bryan and 365 Days of Catch," *The Moonlight Graham Show*, episode 78, September 11, 2018, https://www.stitcher.com/podcast/the-moonlight-graham-show /e/56205965?autoplay=true.

6   W. P. Kinsella, *Shoeless Joe* (New York: Mariner Books, 1999), 98.

high standards and hate sloppiness, and don't suffer fools gladly," the servant replied when the nobleman, now king, returned.

"You're right that I don't suffer fools gladly—and you've acted the fool! Why didn't you at least invest the money in securities so I would have gotten a little interest on it?"

The king gave the money from the fool to the servant who had doubled his funds. "Risk your life and get more than you ever dreamed of. Play it safe and end up holding the bag."

Without risk, there is no reward, only regret.

Without risk, there is no love and no friends.

Without risk, there is no story to tell.

Without risk, dreams never come true.

Without risk, dads don't raise dreamers.

16
Therapy Catch

Hardly anybody recognizes the most significant
moments of their life at the time they happen.
I figured there'd be plenty more days.
—DOC GRAHAM, SHOELESS JOE

"WHO ARE YOU AND WHERE ARE YOU GOING?"

Answering this two-part question was the first assignment for
sophomores taking Mr. Nichols' English class at Kickapoo High
School. I was rather intimidated by the task in front of me. What
sixteen-year-old boy knows who they are? But as I put my thoughts on
paper, I was surprised to start learning about myself, little by little. As
for where I was going, that answer was quite simple. A one-sentence
paragraph: "I am going to play baseball for the Kansas City Royals."

When the paper was returned, a red C-minus was circled at the
top. My pulse tripled and I thought I was going to be sick to my
stomach. I did not feel I deserved to be in Mr. Nichols' class. My
worst fears about teenage me were confirmed: I wasn't good enough.
I stayed after school to see what I did wrong. I can still hear his velvet

bass voice in my ears. "Mr. Bryan, I have no doubt you will one day play for the Royals, but you didn't give equal weight to the two parts of the question. Keep writing, Mr. Bryan, keep writing. You will learn."

In Mr. Nichols' class, we read books and we wrote essays. His three-word writing mantra: "Clear. Concise. Complete." He also taught speedreading. With each passing month, I read slower. It was a gift. Thanks be to God, Mr. Nichols' phone number was listed in the phone book. I can only assume he didn't have caller ID. For every single essay, I called him. I asked question after question after question. He often replied to my questions with questions which were infuriating at the time.

"Mr. Bryan, why do you think that character is important?"

"Mr. Bryan, if you were writing the story, how would you have changed it?"

"Mr. Bryan, why is this book important to our world today?"

His questions helped me continue to think and learn more about me.

"May I speak to Mr. Nichols?" is how I started every phone call.

"This is he," was his consistent reply. Before year's end, he called us and tested our phone etiquette and grammar. It was a simple test, and I knew when my call was coming. After only one ring, I answered the phone that was attached to a wall and stretched the cord as far away from everyone else in my family as possible.

"Is Ethan there?" he asked.

"This is he," I replied.

"You passed the test. I have enjoyed having you in class this year," Mr. Nichols replied.

"I have learned so much."

"Have a good evening, Mr. Bryan."

To this day, every time someone calls and asks to speak to me, I think of Mr. Nichols when I reply. When I discover that they're a telemarketer, I just hang up and don't feel too bad. I think Mr. Nichols would hang up, too.

In his class we read so many books: *Lord of the Flies* and *Animal Farm* and *Of Mice and Men* and even one baseball book—*The Chosen.* He once told me that he reread the assigned books every year, often reading them from cover to cover in one sitting. So I decided to try it. The next book assigned was *A Tale of Two Cities.* By this point, my speedreading skills had tanked. I had to be among the slowest readers he'd ever had. It took the majority of a Sunday and a few hours into early Monday, but I did it.

In Mr. Nichols' class, we had to answer questions out loud about what we were reading, which is how I thought my life was going to end. I could almost see the headline: "Sixteen-Year-Old Has Heart Attack in English Class When Asked to Speak in Front of Others." But he wanted us to find our voices, to always be thinking, and to learn how we best express ourselves.

I think it was the night after the final that about a dozen of us went to TP his house. Destruction of private property is just one way sixteen-year-old boys express affection. He was prepared for our visit and welcomed us inside. He offered us food and drink and then extended the fun.

"We should call someone's parents," he said with a mile-wide smile.

I volunteered my number immediately. I think Mom answered the phone.

"Is Ethan there?"

We were stone silent in the background.

"Mrs. Bryan, there has been some activity taking place at my house tonight and I would like to visit with Ethan first thing tomorrow morning. Will you please pass along my message? Thank you."

He hung up and we laughed and laughed and laughed. When I got home, one of my friends had to help explain to my parents that it really was just a joke.

In 2012, the year my family and I moved back to Springfield after living in Kansas City for a little over a decade, my first book was published, a book full of stories about the Kansas City Royals. Thankfully, Mr. Nichols' phone number was still in the phone book, so I called and asked if we could meet for lunch.

We talked about books and writing and poetry, and he filled me in on the past twenty years of his life. As we parted ways in the parking lot, he gave me a hug. "I am so proud of you," he said.

"I had a good teacher," I said.

"I had the best students."

It should come as no surprise that *Dead Poets Society* is one of my favorite movies. Mr. Keating, played by Robin Williams, is a passionate English professor who inspires students to think and helps a shy student find his voice. For most people, *Dead Poets Society* is just a movie. Those of us who were blessed to take Mr. Nichols' class think otherwise. We learned from a real-life Mr. Keating and were pushed to grow, to ask questions, to learn about ourselves and this phenomenal world in the process. We also found an advocate, a mentor, and a friend.

⚾ ⚾ ⚾

Less than a week after Dad and I went to the *Field of Dreams* movie site, I was back in Springfield cheering on Sophie in her first taekwondo tournament when I got a phone call. Mr. Nichols had passed away.

Mrs. Nichols contacted me and asked if I would be willing to say a few words at his memorial service. Standing just outside a room filled with the cheers and screams of the tournament, I couldn't make a noise. My eyes welled up with tears as I shook my head yes; it took me a few moments to be able to speak.

On the day of the service, on the first day of my birth month, I played catch with Kristen Gammon because I knew she would understand (day #213).

A game of therapy catch, paying tribute to the life and inspiration of Mr. Nichols.

Twenty-five years ago, Kristen was the president of my senior class at Kickapoo High School. She's compassionate and funny and absolutely brilliant. She now helps coach the speech and debate team at Central High School, one of the best speech and debate teams in the country. I was grateful for her presence when Kaylea was on the team, going out of town to compete in tournaments, spending the night away from home. Kristen and I had countless classes together during our four years at Kickapoo. She was quick to speak up and offer her thoughts about whatever we were studying. I always thought she was fearless. My singular goal was to make it through class without saying a single word.

Kristen also loved Mr. Nichols.

"Taking his class made me want to learn, to really learn, not just play the high school game," she said.

I knew exactly what she meant. Mr. Nichols believed in me long before I believed in me.

"He's the reason why I majored in English, the reason why I teach English," Kristen said. "When I became an English teacher, I became a little disillusioned. I couldn't replicate the experience of his class. My respect for what he did professionally increased exponentially. To Mr. Nichols, books were more than just books. Books were insights into life. He encouraged us to find the truth of humanity in the stories we read. We were to think and could agree or disagree. He had such high expectations for all of his students."

We met at Kickapoo to play catch in memory of Mr. Nichols. Playing catch while reliving memories of adolescent fears sounds like a Netflix comedy special starring Amy Poehler and Jerry Seinfeld. In reality, it was like rewatching your favorite movie in which each scene drips with truth and joy, in which the characters are best friends helping you take your first steps in this new world. There was no rush, no hurry. Throws were not displays of power or talent but a continuance of the ongoing, heartfelt conversation.

Therapy catch processes life slowly and intentionally.

A few hours later, the pews of Wesley United Methodist Church were packed, and I saw several familiar faces in the congregation as I sat behind the podium. My heart hammered and I cleared my throat constantly as I fumbled with my notes and waited for my turn in the service, feeling exactly like I felt most times I was asked to speak in Mr. Nichols' class. I told the gathered family and friends about how much Mr. Nichols meant to me. About phone etiquette and the failed attempt to TP his house. About getting a C-minus and calling his house over and over. About reconnecting twenty years after I graduated. To conclude, I pulled up a chair close to the pulpit, stood on top, and exclaimed, "O captain! My captain!"

⚾ ⚾ ⚾

Only a couple of weeks after the service, Aaron Unthank texted me, "Have time for a therapy catch on Thursday?"

His message caught me by surprise. I hadn't expected to see Aaron again.

Two weeks after returning home from the Catch 365 Tour of Hope, Jamie and I took Kaylea and Sophie on a second catch-playing, new-friend-making tour of the United States (days #168–176). Florida was our destination, where Aaron Unthank and his wife, Teri, hosted and entertained us.

On day #170, Aaron wore a Catch 365 T-shirt and treated my family to breakfast before driving us to Jack Russell Park, where he used to coach his son's baseball team. Though his beard may have shades of gray in it and though it's been decades since I actually played in a competitive game, we both felt like teenagers running around on the freshly mowed outfield grass. We played long toss and scooped up grounders and chased down fly balls. Aaron grabbed Pearl, his nickname for the catcher's mitt he used when he played collegiately, and gave me a few pointers for throwing out a first pitch, just in case the Royals called. When we were both thoroughly saturated in sweat, he drove my family to the store for Dr Peppers and snacks, and then dropped us off at the beach so we could cool off.

On July 28, 2018, catch-playing day #209, the same day as Sophie's taekwondo tournament and Mrs. Nichols' phone call, Aaron was in Springfield. While we wore matching Catch 365 T-shirts, he topped his off with a St. Louis Cardinals hat and I wore a powder-blue KC Royals hat. In an open field adjacent to the ballpark home of the Springfield Cardinals, we had our second game of catch in 2018.

"We still haven't practiced turning two," Aaron said.

"Or throws to second base," I added.

Aaron didn't know it at the time, but it was a game of therapy catch for me. We played until it was time for Aaron to load up his car and drive to Nashville, where he was teaching at a music camp.

So when he texted me out of the blue for yet another game of catch, I couldn't make my fingers cooperate fast enough to figure out the details. "I'm in town for my grandma's funeral," he wrote, "and would love to just throw a ball and catch it. Baseball is always there when something or someone else ceases to be."

His words reminded me of the epic speech by James Earl Jones at the end of *Field of Dreams:* "The one constant through all the years, Ray, has been baseball. America has rolled by like an army of steamrollers. It's been erased like a blackboard, rebuilt, and erased again. But baseball has marked the time. This field, this game . . . it's a piece of our past. It reminds us of all that once was good. And that could be again."

Both of my grandmothers have passed away in recent years. I know that empty feeling of missing family, of hearing their laughs and stories, especially around holidays and birthdays. Greatmon's hot tamale pie at Christmas. Riding rollercoasters and learning about Bryan family history with Grandma B. Immediately, I rearranged my calendar, creating time to spend with Aaron.

On day #256, at the same crushed-gravel field where I played catch with Taiki and Shane and Shaun and so many other new friends, Aaron and I started stretching. "Our first game of catch was right across the street," he said. "You in the chair with your ankle propped up on a bucket." I hadn't even made the connection between the two locations. In 2015, just after breaking my ankle, Aaron and I met in person and played catch for the first time. He and I had been baseball-loving internet friends for about a year. It took significant effort to throw anything to Aaron because my left foot was non–weight bearing. Aaron's throws were perfect, right at my chest—pop, pop, pop. There wasn't even a risk of the chair tipping or collapsing in an attempt to catch one of his throws. My throws, however, had Aaron running all over the place. His wife took a picture of me with my foot propped up while gripping the ball. It's one of my favorite pictures.

A lot has happened in the three years between our games of catch, as the winners of the last few World Series can attest: Royals. Cubs. Astros*.[1] A bet on that trifecta would have netted billions. I was grateful to be able to use both of my legs, knees, ankles, and feet for catch playing throughout the year.

We spread out slowly, both making strong and accurate throws—pop, pop, pop. Aaron wore a new Jacksonville Jumbo Shrimp hat he received as a birthday present, the Double-A affiliate of the Miami Marlins. I wore my Royals hat that I received as a Father's Day gift just before heading to Florida.

It took about an hour of catch and conversation and curveballs, of sliders and stories, of leather pops and short hops until we were both

---

1   After learning of their sign-stealing scandal, I feel like the Houston Astros championship of 2017 should have a permanent asterisk by it.

covered in sweat and smiling. Therapy games of catch are not meant to be rushed.

"This—" Aaron gestured to the glove and the baseball and the gravel-covered infield. "This feels normal."

We parted ways and I sent him southbound with a care package of Dr Pepper, old baseball cards, and a prayer for safe travels into the winds and rains of Hurricane Florence.

⚾ ⚾ ⚾

"Who are you and where are you going?" These two unspoken questions were at the heart of almost every conversation with my catch partners. At the beginning of the year, I worried how it would be possible to connect playing catch after the passing of a loved one. Now I know.

We play and honor the stories of those who touched us through the stories we dare to live.

17

The Grand Finale

I want to be remembered as a ballplayer
who gave all I had to give.
—*Roberto Clemente*

After celebrating Christmas, we loaded up the Bryan Family
Millennium Falcon for the final road trip of 2018, finishing the year in
Kansas City. Just in case any of the Royals players were in town and
up for a game of catch.

In 2016, inspired by the Royals World Series championship, local
entrepreneur and sports enthusiast Billy Conway created a couple of
T-shirts and sold them out of Stuey McBrew's, a bar in downtown
Lee's Summit. My favorite one said, "Let that be a lesson to you all,
no one beats Kansas City 30 years in a row."

Through the T-shirts, Billy started meeting new people and got a
kick out of seeing strangers wearing them in random places, like music
festivals in other states.

"It's really cool having people you don't know appreciating something you've made," Billy said as we played on day #364. In March

2017, Billy officially started Squints Apparel, making T-shirts inspired by life in Kansas City and the epic baseball movie *The Sandlot*. Billy's designs celebrated the enormous, eighteen-foot-tall shuttlecocks on the lawn of the Nelson-Atkins Museum of Art as well as *The Sandlot* motto, "Legends Never Die."

In February 1920, Rube Foster founded the Negro National League at the Paseo YMCA in downtown Kansas City. The league started with eight teams, including the historic Kansas City Monarchs. Satchel Paige, Jackie Robinson, Ernie Banks, Elston Howard, and Buck O'Neil all once played for the team. To honor Buck's legacy as an ambassador for baseball, Negro Leagues Baseball Museum president Bob Kendrick started the Buck O'Neil Education and Research Center, which will be housed in the former YMCA building. When it opens, the center will be a state-of-the-art research facility for anyone to use, allowing fans of baseball and history to study the Negro Leagues and their impact on American culture.

In June 2018, vandals broke into the building and destroyed the plumbing, flooding the first floor and basement, damaging the parquet floor in the marquee ballroom. When Billy heard the news, he immediately took action. He designed a special T-shirt and donated all proceeds from the sales to the restoration process.

The T-shirt is a tribute to both *The Sandlot* and Buck O'Neil. In red block letters, the T-shirt reads "Legends Never Die" above a blue pennant with Buck's name on it. Below the pennant is a replica of the KC Monarchs logo. Billy posted pictures of the shirt across social media and waited.

Danny Duffy, Royals southpaw pitcher and friend of Sungwoo Lee, retweeted the effort.

"In four hours, we hit the minimum goal and ended up raising $1,500," Billy said.

Billy and I played our game at an old sandlot ballfield next to a pizza place. I wore my Buck T-shirt and we both wore black PF Flyers shoes. I brought my old Wilson glove and Billy started laughing as soon as he saw it.

"I had my old glove in my hand but decided against it!" he said.

I connected with Billy's story and passion immediately. He loves baseball and found a way to share that love with friends and strangers through wonderful and whimsical T-shirts. After playing catch, I couldn't stop smiling. Part of it was because I had fun hearing Billy's stories and meeting him in person. But I was also excited because there was only one day left in 2018 and I was going to finish the year without needing surgery.

⚾ ⚾ ⚾

Day 365.

I woke up at 6:30 to the sound of rain, one of my least favorite weather obstacles. After getting dressed, putting on the T-shirt that most closely resembled a Buck O'Neil and KC Monarchs jersey, I stuffed multiple changes of clothing into my backpack.

Bring it, rain.

The rain brought it. All day long.

My family and I were staying with Jake and Jen, our former house-mates of years past. Jake graciously volunteered to be my chauffeur, navigating rush-hour traffic and the rain, even driving me past an empty Kauffman Stadium on the way to the day's first game of catch on New Year's Eve.

On the last day of 2018, Dave Darby and I met at the Fox 4 studios in downtown Kansas City for catch. A former collegiate first baseman, Dave has played baseball alongside some of the best Royals players of all time, regularly attending Royals Alumni Fantasy Camp. He also hosts impressive tailgates every year at the K. Dave and I tossed the ball in close (but thankfully dry!) quarters, which helped keep my nerves at bay while I was being interviewed. I also received a personal invitation to Dave's Epic Opening Day Tailgate Experience, which was only eighty-seven days away.

A handshake and a selfie, and Jake and I were off again.

As soon as I climbed back into Jake's car and clicked the seatbelt, a mile-wide smile crossed my face. It stayed for the rest of the day. By day's end, my cheeks were sore from the goofy but earnest grin. I had officially played catch every day for a year. The next five games were merely icing on the cake.

⚾ ⚾ ⚾

The Kansas City T-Bones are part of the Independent Professional Baseball League, the same league as the Chicago Dogs. In September, the T-Bones won their second league championship, beating the St. Paul Saints in a best-of-five series. T-Bones general manager Chris Browne, who got his start in baseball serving as the batboy for the Royals during their 1985 World Series run, welcomed us to T-Bones Stadium and gave me a sneak peek at the championship rings. We played catch on the concourse as the rain continued to fall, flooding the infield. Chris entertained me with stories of Buck O'Neil's at bat in the 2006 All-Star Game that the T-Bones hosted. "He was supposed to walk but couldn't keep from swinging."

I asked Chris what working in baseball has taught him about life.

"Nothing is easy," Chris said. "Keep the dream alive. Plow through and persevere."

Handshake. Selfie. Back to the car.

⚾ ⚾ ⚾

The Kansas City Urban Youth Academy officially opened in March 2018 with the mission of empowering the youth of KC through baseball and softball. The skills the athletes learn at the academy prepare them to be leaders both on and off the field. Darwin Pennye spent five years in the minor leagues. On his twenty-fifth birthday, playing at Charlotte, North Carolina, he celebrated by hitting two home runs and a triple. Drafted by the Pirates, Darwin learned about playing the outfield under the eyes of Bill Virdon. Darwin knows how baseball raises leaders. He's now the executive director of the KCUYA and passes on his wisdom to the next generation. While high school players were practicing turning double plays behind us, Darwin and I played catch on the academy's warm and dry indoor infield, just past the Alex Gordon fence.

"Play every game like it's your last," Darwin said. "The time goes by way too fast."

Handshake. Selfie. Back to the car. This time, however, Jake drove us across town under snowfall.

Big, fat, heavy flakes fell alongside the rain.

⚾ ⚾ ⚾

On the day before he started as an MLB columnist for ESPN, Jeff Passan agreed to catch. He's the author of *New York Times* bestseller *The Arm,* a book describing the epidemic of Tommy John surgeries among professional and amateur baseball players. It took Jeff four years to research and write the manuscript. Stories from that book stayed with me throughout this endeavor. There was always, always a small part of me worrying and waiting for a pop or tear. Jeff writes both from a passion for the game and as a parent of two sons who love to play baseball. I love how Jeff shapes his stories and have read the vast majority of them. His favorite story of 2018, though, surprised me.

"My favorite story was my biggest screwup, saying Shohei Ohtani couldn't hit. It reminds me how fallible I am and how incredible baseball is. Some of the brightest minds in the game can look at someone

and see something and be so incredibly wrong. To me, that encapsu-
lates the beauty of the game."

In the rain and the snow, we played catch. Trying our best to stay
as dry as possible, we played a version of speed catch. My plant foot
landed in a mud puddle and slid and I immediately felt the effects in
my quad and hamstrings. My PF Flyers were soaked and I could not
have cared less. It was a joy to meet and play catch with such a fantastic
baseball writer, even in the rain and the snow and the sloshy mud pits.

Handshake. Selfie. Back to the car.

Jake and I made a quick stop at Chick-fil-A for sustenance and
warmth, and then left for one more game.

No handshakes or selfies. Back to the car.

⚾ ⚾ ⚾

Throughout the year, friends from Kansas City encouraged me and
expressed interest in participating. Just up the road from the Frank
White Jr. Softball Complex, we planned to gather for coffee and
catch. Except the coffee shop closed early. Jake and I were joined
by a host of friends and family. The final game of catch included a
dozen people.

Brenna, Gracie, and Gabe Mueller, the youngest participants of
the day.

Katrina High, a comic artist and librarian.

Brandon Nichols, who works with Squints Apparel to bring Billy's
ideas to life.

Leslie, Alexis, and Sabrina Guyton, friends from my former
church.

Jesse McDaniel, the drummer from my old band.

And, like bookends on the year, Kaylea and Sophie.

After thirty minutes of catch, everyone had wet socks and cold
fingers.

Lots of high fives and hugs. Lots of selfies. And then back to the cars to search for a coffee shop that was open.

⚾ ⚾ ⚾

Late that night, mere hours before 2018 turned into 2019, Nash High came to Jake's house. He'd had to work and hadn't been able to meet for the community game of catch.

"Got time for one more game?" he asked.

With the help of Christmas lights hanging from the gutter and the headlights of the Bryan Family *Millennium Falcon,* we played catch. Nash is a southpaw and a musician, playing and writing for the KC band Tiny Escalators. His dream for 2019 is to continue playing, writing, and growing his music, for music also brings people together in amazing ways. He works for the library in downtown KC and brought me a gift—the end-cap card with the Dewey decimal numbers for a catch-playing book.

"Just a little inspiration for you to write the book," he said.

And with that, Catch 365 was complete.

More than 530 different catch partners.

More than 12,000 miles driven in the Bryan Family *Millennium Falcon.*

Ten states.

Seven really good sliders I threw.

One new glove perfectly broken in and donated to a high-school baseball player.

Countless incredible memories.

⚾ ⚾ ⚾

Playing catch for 365 straight days strengthened and encouraged my sense of curiosity. I felt like *Calvin and Hobbes,* going out on an adventure with friends, making observations, and learning about all of life. Developing a curious mind that seeks to learn from others is imperative in our ever-changing culture.

Playing catch for 365 straight days helped me to live out one of the most important life truths: never give up. Life is hard. It takes courage and grit to do new things, things at which you're not sure whether you'll succeed or fail. It takes tenacity to do anything worth doing. Just because something is hard doesn't mean it's time to give up.

Playing catch for 365 straight days gave me a renewed sense of hope and deep feelings of optimism and wonder. Each day was like opening another present, hearing the stories of that day's catch partner.

Playing catch gave me the best of gifts: experiencing the fullness of life in the present tense.

Afterword

Day #366

Throw.
Catch.
Repeat.
Quixotic all-consuming quest
of daughters, driving, lifelong dreams
of persevering passion
of oh-so-sore muscles and over-the-counter medicine.
Throw.
Catch.
Repeat.
World-class worldview-shaping education
of play and purpose
of road-trip friends and first pitches
of miracles and margin in midst of the mundane.
Throw.
Catch.
Repeat.
Playing into brokenly busy world
discovering beauty present
hidden

creating memories and gathering marbles
with rookies and professionals
of all ages.
Throw.
Catch.
Repeat.
Shattered strings.
Gifted gloves.
Holding hope.
Learning love.
Throw.
Catch.
Repeat.

I HOPE TO MAKE PLAYING CATCH ON NEW YEAR'S DAY A NEW TRADITION. Wearing new tennis shoes and a new Royals hat but taking an old baseball and my older Wilson glove, I drove with my family to Kauffman Stadium to officially ring in 2019. In a 10-degree wind chill, which was a little warmer than it was the previous year, we got our thirty throws in as I dreamed Royals dreams of warmer days ahead. Catch 366?

⚾ ⚾ ⚾

I played catch every day for a year and a day.

Every. Single. Day.

Many days, I played more than once. Some games were "off the record." Some people wanted to play catch without the expectation of a blog post to follow.

I did not need surgery.

I did not secure a glove contract with Wilson.

I did not receive an invitation to spring training with the Kansas City Royals.

But I can wait. I know that dreams that take thirty years to come true end up making the best stories.

I did not keep count of rejections, though I probably should have. I did, however, hold on to the one rejection letter that came through the mail.

Dear Mr. Bryan,

Thank you for inviting President Bush to meet with you for a game of catch. He appreciates your taking the time to inquire.

Unfortunately, President Bush's schedule will not allow for any additional commitments at this time. While we are currently unable to accommodate your request, we will gladly keep it on file in case an opportunity presents itself in the future.

President Bush thanks you for your thoughtfulness. He sends his best wishes.

Sincerely,
Logan Garner
Office of George W. Bush

It's the best form-letter rejection with a presidential seal in the return address I've ever received.

Like any other discipline one undertakes, my brain and body were significantly reshaped. Once I pressed on through the pain of the early weeks, rediscovering muscles that had been dormant for quite some time, I found great joy and purpose in playing catch. The existential weight I felt at the beginning of the year had lifted.

Have gloves. Will travel.

Throw.

Catch.

Repeat.

Acknowledgments

IT WAS EASIER TO PLAY CATCH EVERY DAY FOR 365 DAYS THAN IT WAS to figure out how to write a book about playing catch every day for 365 days and honor everyone who helped make this wonderful year possible.

Thank you, catch partners. With everything in me, thank you. Your time and stories made this year unforgettable. To those who extended invitations and we haven't yet connected, keep your glove handy.

Thank you, Mike King, for connecting me to Mark Oestreicher. Thank you, Marko, for your patient, humor-filled wisdom in helping these stories find a home. Thank you, Andy "Rogers" Rogers, for the prayers and questions and pushing my writing chops. I'm looking forward to our game of catch and know that Marko can't wait to join in. Thank you, Brian Phipps, for making sure my words and stories actually say what I'm trying to say. And thank you to the rest of the Zondervan team for helping this story come to life—Andrea, Alyssa, Bridgette, Trinity. What a joy to work with such amazing people.

Thank you, Mom and Dad, for helping connect me with so many wonderful catch partners and encouraging me throughout this quixotic year.

Thank you, Jamie, Kaylea, and Sophie, for putting up with my quirky ideas, my jump scares, and all of my baseball dreams. I think I'm starting to learn why people care about playing catch. It is a joy to play and live out God's Great Story with you.

Appendix

The Catch 365 Complete Roster

Day #1, Part One—Thirty throws with Sophie, my youngest daughter, in a 1-degree wind chill at Fassnight Field.

Day #1, Part Two—Twenty-five throws with Kaylea, my oldest daughter, in the back yard. It warmed up four degrees and created foggy glasses.

Day #2—On the way to see *Jumanji*, Sophie and I stopped again at Fassnight for thirty more throws.

Day #3—Greg Janssen is a musician and cameraman for the Kansas City Royals and Kansas City Chiefs. *Santa Claus Is Coming to Town* played as background music on the square as we played catch.

Day #4—I've known Andrew Sherrill for decades. Five Januarys ago, he learned he had leukemia. He's been in remission for three years now. We celebrated with lunch-break catch.

Day #5—The first game of catch on video with news anchor Daniel Shedd and photographer Chris Six of KOLR-10/CBS. This story was featured on multiple news stations nationwide.

Day #6—A cosplayer with a passion for charity work and the Cleveland Indians, Springfield's Thor, aka Chris Taylor, played catch in full costume, even though throwing with wrist guards on is ridiculously difficult.

Day #7—Harper Satterfield started bringing his glove to church last year. For us, playing catch is almost sacramental. Sleet clicked off my glasses and my feet slid with every throw.

Day #8—I started playing catch with Dad when I was eight. Now he has arthritis in his hands. For the first time in years, we played catch in the back yard and celebrated Mighty Henry's fourth birthday.

Day #9—Adam Riso watched game 7 of the 2014 World Series from the parking lot of Kauffman Stadium with his daughter. He understands my Royals fandom.

Day #10—Megan Rice is an award-winning sports journalist from Chicago whose big dream for 2018 is getting married in October. "Having a beer with Theo Epstein and getting the chance to interview him would be pretty awesome, too."

Day #11—Chris Brammer is the director of the Springfield Men's Chorus. A cold front passed through during our catch, dropping the temperature considerably, making Chris reconsider his concert plans for that night.

Day #12—The St. Louis Cardinals caravan came to Springfield. Pitcher and World Series champion Kyle McClellan threw perfect curveballs and knuckleballs in front of several witnesses. His nonprofit Brace for Impact 46 is doing amazing work in Haiti and North St. Louis.

Day #13—Nate Reed was accompanied by his dog Lucky. Nate does brilliant work with the Alzheimer's Association. "When you meet the people and hear their stories, you want to help."

Day #14—Church services were canceled because Springfield looked like the White Witch's version of Narnia. So my family and I slowly drove to two locations for catch with Kristie Stoddard, then to the Satterfields' with Harper and his siblings, Atticus and Radley.

Day #15—On the advice of my wife, I asked Jesse Sparks, who works at Johnny Mac's Sporting Goods, to play catch in the indoor hitting tunnel. Jesse, a math student at Missouri State University and a Yankees fan, graciously agreed.

Day #16—Friend, teacher, rapper, BBQ lover, and Royals fan Josh

Kennedy and I met in front of the Royals World Series Champions mural at the Missouri Sports Hall of Fame. The wind chill was minus 15.

Day #17—Wyatt Wheeler is a writer for the *Springfield News-Leader* and wrote one of my favorite stories of 2017, about an eighty-hour charity baseball game. We made new tracks on a snow-covered Fassnight Field.

Day #18—Journalist Jim Connell started writing sports stories just before I got married. A Chicago White Sox fan, he has interviewed Frank Thomas and dreams of interviewing Tiger Woods.

Day #19—Chandler Maples is a biology major at MSU who has played in a game at Hammons Field. He now helps coach the junior high school team in Clever, Missouri. "I knew my playing days were done, but I couldn't get away from baseball. I had to find a way to give back."

Day #20—I grew up going to church with Michael Olmsted, a Cubs fan whose dad was our pastor. We've played catch all over the state of Missouri. Kaylea joined us, and Michael gave her collegiate advice: "Enjoy the process. Whether you're auditioning for a college or playing at church, your most important Audience absolutely delights in you."

Day #21—Harper and Atticus Satterfield, Brennan and Chloe Stoddard, and I gathered on the first day of the week for the breaking of bread, the praying of prayers, and the playing of catch. I'm convinced playing catch is just another way of praying.

Day #22—Cory Goode, a Royals fan and dear friend, agreed to a game of catch to commemorate the one-year anniversary of the death of Yordano Ventura. "The game lives on."

Day #23—Robert Myers is one of those genuine people who accepts people just as they are, who makes all misfits feel welcome and normal. We had cashew chicken followed by catch in the cold.

Day #24—Jeff Kessinger writes for the *Christian County Headliner*. We had lunch on the square in Ozark before catch, and Jeff quoted Ralph Waldo Emerson: "God will not have his work made manifest by cowards."

Day #25—Art Hains is a Royals fan and announcer for the MSU Bears and KC Chiefs Network. His walk-up song: "Joy to the World" by Three Dog Night.

Day #26—Alec McChesney interned with the *Kansas City Star* in 2017 and interviewed several of my favorite baseball players—Salvador Perez, Alex Gordon, and others. He's endured three ACL surgeries.

Day #27—A twilight game with John, Kristin, and Drew "The General" Kessinger. I helped Drew catch a ball with two hands just like Dad used to work with me.

Day #28—Brett from Play OK Antiques sent an old Wilson glove for me to use at the *Field of Dreams*. Owen Hoevet is in Springfield because his daughter attends MSU. I used the new old glove for my first game of catch with a southpaw.

Day #29—Parker Boykin, a senior at MSU studying criminology, works at Johnny Mac's. On a freezing day, we had to get managerial approval for another indoor game of catch.

Day #30—Kevin Agee is the social-media guru and storyteller at Missouri State University and a Royals fan. When Kevin was thirteen, then–KC Royals GM Allard Baird once called him.

Day #31—Coach Keith Guttin is in the Missouri Sports Hall of Fame and has a fantastic resume working with the MSU Bears baseball team, help- ing coach seventeen MLB players. "Every single time life knocks you down, you absolutely have to get back up."

Day #32—Journalist Rance Burger wore a Tulsa Drillers hat and a Mizzou hoodie and likes odd and unusual athletes. My kind of people. He wrote a story of a student from India who played cricket and transitioned to play baseball at Central High School.

Day #33—On the first road trip of the year, Jake Mueller, former housemate, and I found adequate lighting at a skate park in Lee's Summit, Missouri, for the first night game of catch. "The last time I played catch was with you. That was 2011."

Day #34—Bob Kendrick, president of the Negro Leagues Baseball Museum, on the Field of Legends. I stood next to Satchel Paige. He stood by

Josh Gibson and told stories of Buck O'Neil. "Buck would've played catch every day with someone if he'd had the opportunity. He loved the game that much."

Day #35—Matt Burke and Jeff Williams are dear friends and brothers-in-law who skipped out of the circus to join me on the MSU campus and play catch in a blizzard.

Day #36—Elisa Raffa is a graduate of Cornell University, meteorologist, and Yankees fan who once met Derek Jeter. We met at Meador Park on National Weatherperson's Day. Most of the snow from the previous day's blizzard was gone.

Day #37—Jonathan Stratman is a movie-making barista at Mudhouse Coffee. His reaction to learning he has a brain tumor made him internet famous. He asked me to write his obituary, which I did in exchange for catch. "Live caffeinated."

Day #38—Tom Trtan, a journalist and anchor, agreed to play catch and invited me on *Ozarks Live* for my second game on video. He had the idea that I should go to the United Nations and play catch and have conversations with international dignitaries. "Goodwill ambassador of catch playing and storytelling."

Day #39—Brad Beattie played professionally in the Baltimore Orioles organization and works for the Springfield Cardinals. He still plays in the Men's Senior Baseball League. "Through the game, I've learned about leadership and how to be a better person in the community, how to give back and live fully."

Day #40—Kevin Howard and Liz Delany are deejays on 105.9 KGBX, and Matt Parrish is the station manager. A radio interview and a parking-lot game of catch, including a toss into a car with someone just driving by.

Day #41—Keith Kaster taught me the value of perseverance while working in his music studio recording various projects. We played catch in the freezing drizzle before a MSU Bears basketball game and Postmodern Jukebox concert.

Day #42—Aaron Meyer, assistant coach for the MSU Bears baseball team, after listening to Al Hrabosky share stories at the program's annual First Pitch fundraiser. Catch on the artificial green grass behind the facility was similar to playing on an ice skating rink.

Day #43—Derek Edwards, the assistant groundskeeper at Hammons Field, gave me a firsthand education in field maintenance. He was my boss for six weeks before I needed ankle surgery. Another indoor game while Springfield was covered in ice.

Day #44—Don Louzader is the voice of KTTS radio, especially during bad weather. He also holds the course record at Fun Acre Mini Golf. His knowledge of St. Louis Cardinals trivia is vast.

Day #45—On Valentine's Day, a game of catch with my wife, Jamie Bryan, and connecting Catch 365 to raising money for Miracle League in honor of her work with students who have multiple disabilities. $110 was raised while she was at school.

Day #46—The day after another school shooting, I was quite anxious taking my daughters to school. Curtis Satterfield, the youth minister at Hope and Anchor Church, shared verses with me as we played catch. In the words of Buck O'Neil, "Don't let hate fill your heart."

Day #47—Professional photographer Bruce Stidham grew up in England and is a Detroit Tigers fan. After the Houston Astros won the World Series, Bruce took pictures of Bill Virdon, who used to manage for them. Bruce knew that Virdon had even been mentioned in an episode of *Seinfeld*.

Day #48—Mary Ellen Chiles is working on her thesis and is the poet laureate for the MSU Bears baseball team. Cousin of Jerry Lumpe, she hit a home run at Lumpe Field during a Fourth of July family reunion.

Day #49—After playing catch with Harper at church, I drove to Fassnight Field and played catch with two teenagers, Mack and Matthew. As soon as we were finished, they disappeared, oddly reminiscent of Lou Brock's angel story at Southern University.

Day #50—Lael Kennedy is Josh's oldest daughter. She greeted me dressed in all things Royals and we created her own baseball nickname as the wind tried to blow our hats off our heads.

Day #51—Jill Finney is Vice President of Communications for the United Way of the Ozarks. On a horribly rainy day, the YMCA let us borrow a racquetball court for catch and inspiration. When life throws a curveball, don't give up.

Day #52—Jeff Newlin is the owner of Play It Again Sports in Springfield. We played catch between the free weights and stationary bikes, followed by ground ball practice. An errant throw broke a mannequin's hand. Jeff donated a glove for southpaws to borrow that was used throughout the year.

Day #53—Andy Mills, general manager of Lambert's Café in Ozark, Missouri, started out as a roll thrower at the age of sixteen. I did not throw any rolls, just baseballs in the parking lot.

Day #54—Officer Jacob Boomgaarden stands six foot ten. He greeted me in full uniform plus thirty-five pounds of gear and borrowed the glove for southpaws. Giving stickers to kids is his favorite part of the job.

Day #55—Another February deluge fell inducing flash flooding. I was invited to White Brothers Baseball in Fordland, Missouri, where I joined in a practice session with Hunter and Aaron and their twelve-year-old teammates. Hunter graded me: "I'd give you a B. You've got talent."

Day #56—With the help of friends, we planned a surprise birthday party for Kaylea. The co-conspirators—Zoe Young, Carson Marquart, and Sophie Payne—joined me for catch after cake and presents in perfect weather.

Day #57—Kristy Frans is the director of RSVP, a nonprofit agency that engages senior adults in life-changing volunteer work. "Odd projects fit you well. Keep having fun."

Day #58—Nick Warnock is a photographer and an artist and the sound magician from church. We played catch near *The French Fries,* a sculpture that serves as a greeter to the Springfield Art Museum.

Day #59—Liz McCreight is a social-media marketing professional who helps organize the entrepreneurial community of 1 Million Cups, which meets at the art museum. Creating a community of dreamers and creatives is essential for the health of any city.

Day #60—Mack Brown is the quarterback coach for the Missouri State

University Bears football team. I struggled warming up with a football but found my rhythm when we switched to gloves and a baseball. Mack showed me several arm stretches I used throughout the year.

Day #61—In 1955, Bill Virdon won Rookie of the Year with the St. Louis Cardinals. He won the World Series with the Pirates in 1960. I heard the story of Bill's playing in a few games in 1968 after retiring and his only hit being a bottom-of-the-ninth-inning home run.

Day #62—Coach Neil Pittman was my high-school baseball coach, who coached for thirty-six seasons. We played catch at Kickapoo High School outside the field now named for him. I told him thank you for believing in me as a player.

Day #63—AJ Exner played baseball collegiately and later was the very first Strike the Sasquatch, the mascot for the Northwest Arkansas Naturals. At twenty-one months old, his son Benton was one of my youngest catch partners.

Day #64—Clay Engel plays baseball for Drury University. His miracle story involves falling off a mountain cliff, fracturing his skull and vertebrae, and being led by an angel down the mountain to the home of a retired navy medic, who administered first aid and helped him get to a hospital.

Day #65—"I never not know where this glove is," poet Loren Broaddus said of his Bobby Bonds signature model he bought in fourth grade. Now a history teacher at Kickapoo High School, Loren emphasizes the role baseball played in the civil rights movement.

Day #66—In 1964, Coach Bill Rowe was the first coach for the Missouri State Bears. He stayed for nineteen years and then served as the athletic director for the university. "I really like what you're doing, playing catch, being with people. This is a good thing."

Day #67—On International Women's Day, I played catch with Jaimie Trussell, Senior Director of Community Engagement for Convoy of Hope. Jaimie's work has sent her around the world—Kenya, Haiti, Nicaragua, Tanzania, and Ethiopia—advocating for the empowerment of women.

Day #68—Debbie Doherty learned to play catch from Dave, her older brother by thirteen years. His motto, "Learn to catch . . . or die," helped prepare Debbie to be a stellar, two-sport athlete in college.

Day #69—Road trip #2, back to Kansas City. I played catch with Colten Shields, who has Prader-Willi syndrome, and helped him break in his new glove. My family and I fell in love with Colten when Jamie was his first babysitter. He practiced pitching and we watched a spring training game together.

Day #70—Ray plays on the Kansas City Royals wheelchair softball team. At a practice in preparation for the Wheelchair Softball World Series, I played catch (and took swings!) with Ray and two of his teammates. "When the neighbor kid down the street crashes his motorcycle, we want him and others to know we're here."

Day #71—Shayla Patrick is a former collegiate volleyball player at MSU. Now a Fox 4 News reporter in Kansas City, she offered Kaylea advice after her first college visit: "Take risks. Make new friends. And join the weirdest club you can find; you never know what you might learn."

Day #72—Caleb Leaders is my cousin's son and was in Springfield for his brother's homeschool basketball tournament. He lives big and wears his scars proud. We threw pop-ups while his siblings watched from the swings.

Day #73—Tim Clegg is the founder of Hurts Donut Company, which he opened with less than seven dollars in his bank account. The doors have never closed. A former GM of the Ozark Mountain Ducks, he now uses his position to help raise money for the Multiple Sclerosis Society.

Day #74—Caleb Davis is a friend from church and plays baseball at Central High School. He was born in Kazakhstan, helped his parents plant a church in Hawaii, and is a sidearm pitcher who speaks softly but throws big breaking balls.

Day #75—Kirk Elmquist is the director of the Bass Pro Shops Legends of Golf tournament at Big Cedar Lodge. He used to work in the front office for the Springfield Cardinals and is responsible for first hiring their current GM. "Be aggressive. Don't give up. Find a way to get to the people you need to get to. Don't be afraid to ask for help."

Day #76—Addi is a miracle. It took sixteen years for her condition to be diagnosed as TRAF7 syndrome. There are only twenty known cases in the world. Addi is a multisport athlete and is pretty much ambidextrous.

Day #77—Bill Cantrell is a friend from college who gave me a Jon Jay autographed bat, now that Jay plays for the Royals. Bill dreams of starting a podcast where everyone can share their stories, because sharing stories creates community and hope.

Day #78—Tyler is a life coach at I Pour Life, a nonprofit that helps young people transition into adulthood. "When you are pushed outside your comfort zone, that lack of comfort creates big opportunities, if you're willing to put in the time and work. A true coach is someone who willingly sets their agenda aside to listen and help another person become better. And so much of coaching is applicable to all parts of life."

Day #79—Local pastor and Baltimore Orioles fan Phil Snider has survived going viral and passionately advocates on behalf of the poor and culturally marginalized. Phil also coaches his son's baseball team, so he has a bucket of baseballs and a fungo bat in his truck at all times. In the grass lot behind his church, he hit me fly balls after we played catch.

Day #80—Joe Murano is a New York Yankees fan who works the sunrise shift as an anchor for the Springfield CBS affiliate, KOLR-10. Joe is quite well-traveled and is enjoying settling into the community, meeting new neighbors, and running the trails throughout the Midwest.

Day #81—Oklahoma lawyer Josh Payton is one of my first best friends. A bird dog scout, Josh once clocked me throwing 71 mph. He's now working on a nonprofit to help those in the minor leagues make a sustainable wage as they play ball.

Day #82—One of Luke Lohman's throws finally broke the strings on my George Brett glove. We laughed and I caught the rest of his throws on the palm. Even if he cheers for the Cardinals, Luke is my kind of guy. "Playing catch was definitely the high point of my day."

Day #83—Lauren Barnas is a news anchor on the Daybreak Team

for KOLR-10. She brought Jaxx, her German shepherd, with her to catch. Lauren's love of Springfield philanthropy sent her "Over the Edge," rappelling down the side of a building to raise money for the Child Advocacy Center.

Day #84—Riley Hesterly is a three-sport athlete: basketball, track, and baseball. He takes pride in his pitching and has a good fastball. Riley is a huge fan of his Special Olympics teams, and he annoys his older sister only some of the time.

Day #85—I played catch with Kendi Satterfield at the birthday party of a mutual friend three years ago. A year later, my family started attending the same church as Kendi and her family. From Ohio, Kendi played pretty much every sport in high school. She now is on the leadership team at church and advocates on behalf of children with severe emotional and behavioral needs.

Day #86—Dr. Kayla Lewis is a professor and graduate literacy program coordinator at Missouri State University. It was as we played catch that I learned she is also Chickasaw. "I see diversity and the need for diversity everywhere. I intentionally incorporate multiculturalism in all I do. As a literacy professor, I have the joy and responsibility of doing it through books."

Day #87—Tammy Flippen is the organizer of events and chaos at The Library Center, specializing in grants and community involvement. A talented resource librarian, Tammy helped me research for *Dreamfield*. Thanks to a never-ending sense of humor, Tammy has survived six ankle surgeries.

Day #88—On MLB's opening day, I did a baseball poetry reading to more than two hundred fifth graders. After poems and stories, I used my brand-new Wilson glove to play catch with several students in Josh Kennedy's fifth-grade class.

Day #89—John Sellars is the executive director of the History Museum on the Square. John shared multiple stories of Springfield history and its impact and importance today. "What we need to do is put our arms around one another and commit to making the future brighter and better. Together."

Day #90—Like me, Joel Gammon has alopecia. I constantly remind and tease him about wearing hats and sunscreen at all times. While Joel was playing second base last summer, a ground ball took a bad hop and went in the sleeve of his jersey. Life is all about adapting to the bad hops.

Day #91—On Easter, it was still cold. Spring had not sprung. Kaylea and Sophie played catch with me before church and agreed to an interview. "Putting yourself out there and trying is important because you never know where it will get you," Kaylea said. "Hang in there, hopefully it's going to get warmer soon," said Sophie.

Day #92—Andrew Sherrill and his eight-year-old son, Lucas, met me at the Miracle League field in the dense fog for a slippery game of catch on the artificial field. We kept playing as the sun set, and Lucas was hurt on an errant throw (by me) caused by the slippery surface. He drew me a picture of a baseball as a sign of his forgiveness.

Day #93—Jamie Kessinger and her two-year-old twin sons, Romey and Finnegan, played catch with me in their back yard. After years in restaurant management, Jamie followed in her family's footsteps of styling hair. Her boys, while identical twins, preferred to throw the ball with opposite hands. Catch was followed by high fives and the blowing of bubbles.

Day #94—Kendal Dingus is one of Springfield's 40 Under 40. A banker with a corner office and three computer screens, he is also a remarkable artist who transforms barn wood into all kinds of amazing furniture.

Day #95—Marty Prather is known around St. Louis Cardinal and Missouri State nations as The Sign Man. The owner of multiple Domino's Pizza stores, he makes signs for every game he attends. He greeted me with my own sign: "Wanna play catch?" Marty was elected into the Missouri Sports Hall of Fame because of his superfandom.

Day #96—Chris Donegan has been playing softball since before we attended college together. Doing all things with a smile on his face, he still plays weekly as well as umpires. "It's just fun being on the field, you know?"

Day #97—After a mid-April snow, Sarah Sparkman, better known as Cupcakes, led me in a series of yoga stretches before catch. A brilliant lawyer, Sarah is a passionate fan of the Royals and the Northwest Arkansas Naturals. Sarah advocates on behalf of victims of domestic battery and abuse, helping them to receive a fair resolution and find the resources they need to begin the healing process and move forward.

Day #98—"My glove is always in my car," Sarah Odom said. "I think it's a sign of hope." A middle-school principal, Sarah has spent two decades in public education and knows about the importance of both play and hope. After a morning of April snow, Sarah encouraged me: "This too shall pass."

Day #99—Jennifer Johnmeyer, the creative manager at Alamo Drafthouse Movies, organized a screening of *Field of Dreams* to benefit Springfield's Miracle League. We filled 90 percent of the theater, which helped support fourteen players. W. P. Kinsella would have been proud.

Day #100—Ryan Wolfe is the general manager of CY Sports Center, an indoor baseball training facility. A faithful encourager and supporter of Catch 365, Ryan found me several catch partners throughout the year and provided indoor space when the weather turned bad. I cheered him on as he played in the Grip 'N' Rip Baseball League.

Day #101—I celebrated a birthday game of catch with Bill Shedd, who recently retired after spending thirty-nine years working in radio. I did not know it was his birthday or else I would have brought birthday donuts. Bill also spent a decade coaching youth baseball teams. "I love working with younger people and teaching them the right way to play the game—about respect for the game, for teammates, for coaches, and for opponents. In return, I learned a lot about patience! But it sure was a lot of fun."

Day #102—Emily Hall is a paraprofessional teacher at Delaware Elementary working toward earning her master's degree in special education from Drury University. "These kids have definitely changed my life. The joy they have is contagious. By no means is the job easy, but it is so rewarding."

Day #103—At The Barn at Belamour, a premier wedding venue north of Springfield, I played catch with Kim Bell on the birthday of her late husband, Howard. Kim's heart for hospitality has found its best expression and purpose in celebrating love. Kim gave an acceptance speech when Howard was inducted into the Missouri Sports Hall of Fame.

Day #104—Justin Glazier used to work for the Springfield Cardinals and the Tacoma Rainers and is now working toward a master's degree in project management. Justin and I survived cold, whipping winds and a neighbor's dog, who interrupted our game of catch multiple times.

Day #105—Lester Ratcliff is an umpire who dreamed of working a district championship game. (His dream came true.) Lester moved to Springfield to run track and play football at MSU. On Jackie Robinson Day, Lester emphasized the importance and effects of Jackie's legacy seventy years later.

Day #106—Sterling Huff encourages entrepreneurs. At the weekly meetings of 1 Million Cups, he provides space and feedback helping those who are starting their own business find their way forward. "My favorite part is watching the connections take place that happen only in an environment where entrepreneurs ask for help and are willing to learn so they can better shape whatever they are working toward."

Day #107—Larry Flenoid declared April 17 "417 Day" and threw a party. While the event staff prepared for the free neighborhood party, we played catch. "There's so much in this world that causes division, I just felt called to pour my heart into loving neighbors and my community. You have to choose to celebrate what's good. Take a risk and do something that brings people together."

Day #108—Chandler Maples (day #19) invited me to spend time with the Clever Middle School baseball team. Long toss with Dylan and Carson and pop flies and hitting the cutoff man and batting practice: it was a perfect day on the field.

Day #109—Matt Morrow is the president and CEO of the Springfield Area Chamber of Commerce. "This is a great community and there are unlimited opportunities for both entrepreneurs and existing businesses to grow. The people of Springfield are quite special. Their attitude and approach to life exemplify the best about life in the Midwest."

Day #110—I taught Kaylea and Sophie how to catch pop-ups. Just like life, catching pop-ups is all about persistence and perspective, overcoming the fear of getting hurt and trusting your skills.

Day #111, Part 1—Twenty years ago, Patrick Stewart and I met on the campus of MSU at the Baptist Student Union. He first encouraged me to pursue vocational ministry when I was a freshman in college. He now helped me prepare for life as my oldest daughter is thinking about college. Friends are a gift from God.

Day #111, Part 2—Taking a break from math homework, Kaylea wanted to play catch and asked questions about baseball and life after high school.

Day #112—Bethany Kennedy sang songs about the power of love and hope during our church's worship service. A fiercely competitive board-game player and Royals fan, she braved rain and avoided puddles in a quick game of catch before lunch.

Day #113—Ashlynn is a slugger for her Miracle League team. Before the game, she had a track meet and competed in shot put, the 100-meter dash, and javelin throw. She won a gold and two silver medals. Everyone cheered when Ashlynn stepped up to the plate and hit a line drive off the left-field fence.

Day #114—In the same year as his twentieth wedding anniversary, Adam Lawrence filed for and was granted disability. "When people ask me what I'm thankful for, I always say disability. Through it I've found my calling to serve others and give back to the community." Adam now volunteers at a food pantry serving three hundred people each month.

Day #115—Because of a deluge, every baseball game in southwest Missouri was canceled. Nick Francis volunteered to brave the rain for catch. Nick has lived around the world teaching English as a missionary. An entrepreneur and a handyman, he now helps friends find affordable housing through repairing and renting houses.

Day #116—I did a storytelling for Matt Burke's eighth-grade class at Reed Academy and answered their questions about playing catch, living a good story, and chasing dreams. I invited the whole class for a game of catch. Several participated in wearing a glove and throwing a ball for the first time.

Day #117—Dustin Langston is a motorcycle-loving drummer and realtor. His teammate in the house-hunting world is Joseph Keil, who took pictures and videoed via drone while we played catch outside their office. "Life is good. Let's make it better."

Day #118—On the way to hearing Kaylea play in the state music contest, Jamie and I stopped in Lebanon for lunch and catch with Tanner Angst. Tanner is a sophomore at the University of Missouri studying business with dreams of being the GM of a major league team. "Not everything in life is going to go your way. Whenever the odds are against you, you have to keep battling and trust that all of the hard work you've put in will, someday, pay off."

Day #119—Wearing matching Salvador Perez T-shirts, I played catch with my nephew, the Mighty Henry, who wore his favorite orange glove. Kaylea and I practiced knuckle curveballs afterward, then Henry and I cooled off and shared a Dr Pepper.

Day #120—After I presented at 1 Million Cups, James Bonds pulled me aside and prayed for my arm. An impeccably dressed life coach and motorcycle racer, James's mission is to bring hope and healing to the world, equipping people for life today and tomorrow, creating space in which they might live purposeful and focused lives.

Day #121—Larissa Breshears is passionate about sharing stories of those living on life's margins and coordinates the 7 Billion Ones project. While Randy Bacon took pictures, we played catch and Randy told me of the inspiration behind the project. "What I'm learning from my story and sharing the stories of others is that this day is meant to be magical. No matter what happens during the day, it will be filled with moments of blessing and inspiration. You just have to look for them."

Day #122—An early morning Rotary Club storytelling connected me to Will. Will is a southpaw who coaches his daughter's team. He shared stories of Stan Musial and Buck O'Neil as we played catch near the eighteenth green of Twin Oaks Country Club.

Day #123—Dan Reiter is the general manager of the Springfield Cardinals. His job is to create space where families and friends make memories while enjoying the game. "I work in baseball because I absolutely love this game, but several times you have to step back and remove the fan from the businessperson. Baseball is teaching me that everyone needs to have more fun. In general, we need to lighten up and work on having more fun."

Day #124—"College baseball literally saved my life," said Ben Goss. At a Stetson University game, Ben suffered an idiopathic ventricular tachycardia. Now a professor at Missouri State and an announcer for the Bears baseball team, Ben travels the country each summer visiting baseball stadiums and hearing baseball stories.

Day #125—Ken Teague was born to love baseball. "I was named Kenton, after Cardinals Gold Glove All-Star Ken Boyer." Now an insurance agent, he brought his family of St. Louis Cardinals fans to Doling Park to play catch, and he told me about his epic spring training trip: nine stadiums in six days.

Day #126—At my church's annual May Day Soiree Grill Some Food and Come and Play event, several friends joined me in catch before and after lunch, including young southpaw Henry Haynes shortly before he had to leave for baseball practice.

Day #127—Jamie's class took a field trip to the Miracle League field. I brought gloves and appropriate baseballs and played catch with several of her students. One of them laughed every single time he threw and caught the ball. Throw. Laugh. Catch. Laugh. Repeat. It was wonderful.

Day #128—Jay Fotsch is a deejay and an emcee for the Springfield Cardinals. After I sang a horrible rendition of Taylor Swift's "Shake It Off," we played catch in the Power 96.5 studio while on the air, successfully dodging microphones, lights, and mixers. Jay's fiancee is a Royals fan, and she called in to the show in my support. "Baseball is more than just a game."

Day #129—Dustin Stewart works across the street from the Do Good mural off of Commercial Street in Springfield. In 2015, on the day after Christmas, his farmhouse was struck by lightning and burned to the ground. His wife was five months pregnant with their second child when the lightning hit. Now a woodworker, Dustin crafts and designs beautiful furnishings.

Day #130—Jim "The Rookie" Morris had a Disney movie made about his life's incredible journey. At Kauffman Stadium, he gave me advice about never giving up on dreams. "Life is never going to stop throwing things at you.

How you choose to react determines whether you grow or give up. God took me, the person least likely to be a speaker, and turned him into a storyteller."

Day #131—Noble Bowman serves as the chaplain for the Missouri State University softball team. "Every journey, every story, every dream is filled with obstacles. If you're willing to pay the price, those obstacles are just a stop on the way to your ultimate destination. If you're willing to pay the price. The choice is always yours."

Day #132—The Fighting Jackalopes softball team was resurrected. Josh Kennedy, Bethany Kennedy, Jesse Kennedy, Dustin Langston, Barbie Langston, John Kessinger, Kristin Kessinger, Luke Caddy, and Ollie Kessinger invited me to practice.

Day #133—On Mother's Day, before church and not just wearing a T-shirt, I played catch with Mom (Sheri Bryan) and gave her a small bouquet of flowers.

Day #134—Robyn Fondren is the counselor at Delaware Elementary. A Royals fan, she was awarded Elementary Counselor of the Year and encourages big dreams. "Go for it. No matter what happens, you'll find support along the way. No matter what the outcome is, you'll be one step closer to your goal, and you'll learn things on the journey, too."

Day #135—Stephen Herzog is a writer and storytelling coach for the *Springfield News-Leader*. A recovering sports reporter, Stephen was working on an end-of-the-school-year story about the influence of teachers. "I love being able to influence change."

Day #136—Former Springfield mayor Bob Stephens grew up just a few blocks away from our catch-playing venue. "When I'm driving past a ballfield and the lights are on and the dust is hanging over it, my car keeps trying to turn in!" Bob gave me my first lesson in politics. "If someone wants to give you credit for doing something good, even if you didn't do it, take it."

Day #137—Steve Lael and Don Garner coached together at Branson High School and have accrued five combined decades of baseball wisdom through fungos and fastballs. "No transfer of blame," said Coach Garner.

"You accept responsibility for what you do or don't do." "You learn to get over failure, find the good in it, and move on. Baseball's better than football because you get to play the next day. There's always another at bat coming," said Coach Lael.

Day #138—Daniel Shedd followed up his interview on day #5. In a good story, characters are changed through conflict and struggle. He asked the question that stayed with me for the rest of the year. "How is playing catch changing you?"

Day #139—Stephen replaced the shattered windshield in the Bryan Family *Millennium Falcon*. As a teenager, he got involved with the wrong crowd and spent two years in prison. He changed his life and is now pursuing a degree with dreams of being an autonomous vehicle engineer. "Making mistakes is an opportunity to learn. I learned and I changed."

Day #140—Between spring storms, Dad, Kaylea, and I had a three-generation game of catch in the same back yard where I learned how to throw a curveball.

Day #141—Michael Vincent used to be a catcher in the Cincinnati Reds organization, winning the 1985 Double-A Eastern League championship with teammates Rob Dibble, Chris Sabo, and Barry Larkin. Pete Rose and Johnny Bench he knew as coaches. Michael has played ball in thirty-six states and five countries.

Day #142—Played catch with Little Bear of the Beijing Shougang Eagles at U.S. Baseball Park.

Day #143, Part 1—Played catch with Stephanie Young, principal at Delaware Elementary School.

Day #143, Part 2—Played catch with Simone Wearne, who was working with the Aussie Spirit. Simone is the only female inducted into the Australian Baseball Hall of Fame.

Day #144—Darrin Bell and Jake Bell after Howard Bell was inducted into the Missouri Sports Hall of Fame.

Day #145—Brett Kesinger and Bo Kesinger at Kauffman Stadium.

Day #146—Mike Engel at the charity softball game.

Day #147—Leksi Macan and her softball team at a Memorial Day tournament.

Day #148—Martie Cordaro, the general manager of the Omaha Storm Chasers in Omaha, Nebraska.

Day #149—Nathan Rueckert, the president and founder of the Baseball Seams Company in Sioux Falls, South Dakota.

Day #150—Ryan Cellan, who volunteers to maintain a field in his back yard in Wallingford, Iowa.

Day #151—Bigby Suddarth, who has endured multiple heart surgeries in his first three years of life, and his dad, Tim.

Day #152—Mary Moore, a player in the All-American Girls Professional Baseball League, and umpire Perry Barber in Rockford, Illinois.

Day #153—Shane Lamie and Shaun Lamie at Millennium Park in Chicago, Illinois.

Day #154—Kaylea and Sophie in center field at Impact Field, the home of the Chicago Dogs.

Day #155—Brandon Rollwagen works for the Arc of the Ozarks, helping individuals with disabilities live as contributing members of the community. Brandon coordinated a high-fiving, compliment-filled game of catch with his son, Gunnar, and client Eli.

Day #156—Formerly dead person from day #124, Ben Goss is starting a new baseball-themed T-shirt company, Long Ball City. He gave me a T-shirt honoring George Brett's pine-tar home run of 1983.

Day #157—Adam Robles is from Daytona Beach, Florida, but was working in St. Louis. He woke up at 5:00 a.m. to drive to Springfield to play catch before driving back to St. Louis to board his flight home. "You've gotta grind it out. You just don't know what's going to happen. Adapt to life's curveballs. Wait for the break, and take your swing."

Day #158—Cyrus Taylor is the commissioner of Springfield's Miracle League, which started in 2010 with thirteen players. There are 213 players signed up to play this season. "Miracle League is a consistent reminder of what's important in life. We are able to provide everything good about baseball, all the fun aspects, giving anyone who wants to play the opportunity to hit the ball, run the bases, and touch home plate for their team." Every child deserves a chance to play baseball.

Day #159—Trent Sims is the director of development at Springfield's Victory Mission, a faith-based nonprofit that focuses on long-term reconciliation, rehabilitation, and reentry into society. "I really think God works with us to do good in this world, and there's great freedom in that."

Day #160—A mistyped number and text message connected me to Sarah Semple, the director of information technologies for Keller Williams. "I live my life like improv. I say, 'Yes, and . . . ,' then see what happens. So many amazing and unique opportunities open up when you have the courage to say, 'Yes, and.'"

Day #161—Ava Rollwagen and Carolina Kessinger are stepsisters and catch-playing rookies. Ava loves to read and would like to be a doctor; Carolina is fascinated by dance and would like to be a teacher. A Sunday afternoon catch in the shade of a tree after a Springfield cashew chicken lunch is a practically perfect way to spend an afternoon.

Day #162—Mike Essick has been the head coach of the Ozark High School baseball program for twenty-four years. His record is 449–210 and includes two state championships, six district championships, and fifteen Central Ozark Conference titles. "Pay attention and this game will teach you everything, especially during adversity. It reveals your character quickly and emphasizes self-control. It's a game about making the most from what you have been given."

Day #163—I woke up at 5:45 a.m. to play catch with tailgate specialist Mark Menard. Mark is an old soul who smiles and finds the silver lining through all of life's struggles and trials. He is helping umpire games for kids in KC. "It's purely volunteer work, and anytime parents complain, I tell them we could always use more volunteers."

Day #164—Jeff Houghton is the creative force behind Springfield's own Emmy Award–winning late-night talk show, *The Mystery Hour*. He's also the originator of the Instagram Husband concept. "You don't have to believe the fallacy that there are places for dreamers and it's far away from where you are now."

Day #165—Isaiah Goodwyn asked a bold question: "Can I have your glove?" Asking bold questions should always be encouraged. Near the end of Catch 365, just like the Wilson Sporting Goods Company gave me the glove, I passed on the perfectly broken-in glove as a late birthday gift to Isaiah, hoping to inspire more baseball dreams in the next generation.

Day #166—John Miller turned his childhood passion into a paying job. "I saw these guys on TV and listened to them on the radio and it struck me that they were getting paid to watch sports and help bring the game to other people." He now does play-by-play work for Drury University, calling games of all varieties: basketball, soccer, volleyball, baseball, and softball.

Day #167—On his thirteenth birthday, Beau Warren was playing in a baseball tournament for the SEMO War Eagles and hit a home run. "Keep your head up when you win and when you lose, and encourage your teammates."

Day #168, Part 1—On Father's Day, which was also Jim Huntsinger's fiftieth birthday, we played catch and ate donuts. Jim drove 611 miles to connect with me. "There's just so much negativity in this world, on the news every day. And you were playing catch to have fun and to connect with people. I thought it was cool and wanted to be a part of it."

Day #168, Part 2—We drove 525 miles to connect with David Dollar and his son Campbell in Birmingham, Alabama. David knows about the importance of play, helping create magic for families headed to Disney World. "I love helping people who have no idea what they are doing have an incredible, unforgettable vacation."

Day #169—Rickwood Field in Birmingham, Alabama, is the oldest professional baseball field in the United States. Dan played catch and gave me a tour of all the famous ballplayers who have stepped foot between the lines. "More than 175 players in the Hall of Fame have played baseball at Rickwood," Dan told me. "More than any other stadium." Bill Virdon played a few games here in 1953.

Day #170—In Jacksonville, Florida, Aaron Unthank treated us to breakfast at Dano's Diner, where the Colonel warmed me up with catch after filling my belly with fantastic fare. At the field where he used to coach his son Eli, Aaron and I played catch and chased pop-ups and practiced first pitches. Aaron is a musician, and his song "Courageous" served as a theme song for the trip.

Day #171—The Daytona Tortugas were the very first MiLB team to reach out and extend a catch-playing invitation. Playing at Jackie Robinson Ballpark, built in 1914, the Daytona Tortugas are the Class-A Advanced affiliate of the Cincinnati Reds. Luke Mauro is the radio broadcaster for the Tortugas and coordinates all the social media. "On March 17th of 1946, this was the field where Jackie played his first game as a member of the Dodgers organization."

Day #172—Before we visited the Wizarding World of Harry Potter at Universal Studios, Kaylea, the only member of Ravenclaw House in my family, played catch with me just outside our hotel room. "As I think about the books and the series, some of the thoughts that have really stuck with me are the importance of real friends who stick with you and that love is the strongest power."

Day #173—Before our second day indulging in all things Harry Potter, Sophie, a proud Hufflepuff, played catch with me. "Hufflepuffs are known for being kind and loyal, and this world really needs people who practice being kind and loyal every day. The main theme you see throughout all the books is the power of love. It's the first lesson you learn about at the end of the first book and ties together the whole series. Love never fails."

Day #174—In Valdosta, Georgia, sportswriter Derrick Davis connected me with Chris Hetrick and his son, Cameron. A helicopter mechanic in the air force, Chris has coached Cameron's baseball team for several seasons. "Baseball is a game of the meeting of the simple and the complex. I can explain the basics to you in just a couple of minutes, and we can spend a lifetime studying and learning all the nuances."

Day #175—Collin Cunningham is my sister's neighbor. A fan of

Derek Jeter, Collin is a third baseman and pitcher for the Conway High School baseball team, and we spread out across his front lawn to play catch. "Baseball's taught me that there are no shortcuts."

Day #176—Bill Patterson is an optometrist and the founder of the Conway Braves program in Conway, Arkansas, which is similar to Miracle League. My nephew Henry has played ball through this program in past seasons. At age eight, Bill's son, Ben, was discovered to have neurodegeneration with brain iron accumulation. "Kids like Ben are constantly going to doctors, all the different therapists and appointments, but on the ballfield, they can really be a kid."

Day #177—Matt Wilkie is Field Teams Director for international-aid nonprofit Convoy of Hope. Haiti, East Africa, Philippines, and Central America—Matt has truly seen the world. "The hardest part of travel, of course, is being away from my family, but I am thankful to have their support. The best part is the people I meet around the world."

Day #178—On his birthday, in a heat index of 105, Drew Boone and I celebrated with catch. Gifted with an excellent sense of humor, Drew said, "As I've gotten older, I've become more pragmatic. I hope my car makes it to the end of the year."

Day #179—On his birthday, which is also the birthday of his son, at Springfield Catholic High School, where he works, I played catch with Baltimore Orioles fan Dante Rebori, who once sat in the dugout with the Orioles before they played a game in Kansas City.

Day #180—Brent Parker is the general manager of the University Plaza Hotel. On the building's rooftop, nine stories high, we played catch. Sometimes you need a change of perspective.

Day #181—Professional baseball players run in Emilio's family. Emilio Vela Jr. is a consultant and CEO for nonprofit organizations, helping these organizations do their best work. "Get involved! Change happens only by those who have the courage to get involved. We tell stories to empower people to get involved, to give back, to teach others to use their voices. It's about the people, always the people. Not the budgets or bottom line but advocating for and with people so they can live good lives, so they, too, can give back."

Day #182—For the very first time in our lives, I played catch with my sister, Katy Oswalt. We have video proof.

Day #183—At the halfway point, Ann Willingham gave me a history lesson in Springfield baseball, including Branch Rickey, Stan Musial, and Mickey Mantle. An expert in making chocolate-chip cookies, she still plays catch with kids in her neighborhood and enjoys cheering for the major leaguers when they make rehab assignments in Springfield.

Day #184—For Andrew Sherrill's thirty-third birthday, we played catch and he informed me of his move to Kansas City. "I didn't want to grow old and look back at my life wishing I'd done a better job of doing the good work God's got planned for me. I knew now was the time to go all in."

Day #185—Owen Wilkie is a writer and southpaw celebrating his seventy-third birthday on the Fourth of July. With his son and grandson, we played catch and shared stories of the writing life. "I really do love to write, to pass along the wisdom and what God has taught me through story."

Day #186—Joey Mellows spent 2018 traveling the world to watch and learn about baseball. "The best part of this year, besides watching all the games, is getting to know the people, seeing the joy that fans are getting from the game. It's easy to get stuck in a rut. Sometimes, you just have to take a chance and see what happens."

Day #187—The Muellers visited Springfield, turning my home into sleeping quarters for eleven people. Jake Mueller and his oldest son, Gabe, joined Sophie and me for catch at the park. Gabe described playing catch as "epic," which I took as the highest of compliments.

Day #188—Jacob Brazeal is diligently working toward the rank of Eagle Scout. A freshman at Central High School, he created a fundraiser to restore Grant Beach Park. "I know it sounds big, but I want to raise $30,000 to improve this field, so kids have a good place to play baseball and their parents can watch." By day's end, he had raised more than $3,600.

Day #189—A former pitcher at Crowder College and Missouri Southern,

Ryan Verfurth organized a golf tournament to raise funds on behalf of his five-year-old nephew, who was undergoing treatment for stage 4 neuroblastoma at St. Jude Children's Hospital in Memphis, Tennessee. We played catch by the putting green before Dad and I competed in the tournament.

Day #190—With Jamie and Sophie out of town, Adam and Josh Lawrence connected with me and Kaylea for catch at the park. We spread out around the infield. The various distances and great disparity in height made playing catch an adventure in depth perception. Kaylea and I grabbed Dr Peppers on the way home. My bottle said, "Crave adventure."

Day #191—On day #6, before I had any idea what I was doing or what this project would become or where it would take me and my family, I played catch with Springfield's Thor. Today I played catch with his alter ego, Chris Taylor. Like Mr. Incredible, Chris also works in insurance, and his true gift is bringing smiles to people of all ages. Friends who are also superheroes are in short supply.

Day #192—Dan Ponder is a political science professor at Drury University specializing in presidents. But the St. Louis Cardinals fan quickly confessed, "If I could have done anything, I would have been a baseball player."

Day #193—Craigery Tucker, a friend from college at MSU, played catch with me on the hottest day in Springfield in the last four years. Craigery entertained me with his crazy story of traveling to play golf on the Old Course at St. Andrews. There is a certain kind of beauty in daring to do something crazy.

Day #194—Janelle Reed loves tacos and founded Single Momz Rock, a ministry birthed after she went through a divorce while raising two daughters. "Don't ever give up—you never know what's around the corner."

Day #195—Brian Brown went to California to be a sportswriter and almost signed up for a cultlike vegan-only community. He returned to Springfield, met his wife, started writing for *Springfield Business Journal*, considered becoming a political columnist, resigned because of a mystery illness, worked at a cemetery, and wants to try his hand at stand-up comedy.

Day #196—The same day Kaylea was touring cathedrals in Europe, I played catch with Heather. In the past year, Heather Whitford traveled the world as a missionary, crossing three continents and a dozen countries. "I could eat anything once."

Day #197—With both daughters away from home, Jamie and I took a day trip to Bennett Spring State Park and almost hiked into a deer. On the way home, we stopped in Lebanon for catch at the same ballpark where I met Tanner (day #118).

Day #198—Eli Ponder is a student at Central High School and the catcher on the baseball team. He walked me through the team's warmup procedures and let me practice pitching. Then we switched places and I caught his pitches.

Day #199—Rance Burger (day #32) volunteered his time and talent at a sports camp at Kingsway United Methodist Church. He invited me to come and tell stories of baseball and faith and agreed to pay me to play catch. After a story and multiple versions and rounds of catch, I had earned my pay: an ice-cold Dr Pepper.

Day #200—At Glenwood Park, in the midst of noisy construction and overcast skies, and with a toddler mesmerized by our skills, financial advisor and former rugby player Russ Pendleton and I played catch. Playing catch emphasizes living life fully in this moment, even amid all the distractions.

Day #201—After Sophie spent a week washing dishes, fixing meals, cleaning cabins, and going on a float trip, Jamie and I took a day trip to pick her up from Logan Valley Christian Retreat. I played catch with the founder and owner, Dave Williams. In a heat index of 110, the Cardinals fan and I sweated and swapped stories where the camp's softball field used to be.

Day #202—Sarah Buxton is passionate about Jesus, serving others, and politics. Having learned at age fourteen that she has alopecia, she faces each day with a heart full of hope and courage whether or not there is hair on her head.

Day #203—Aaron Davis planted a church in Hawaii before moving back to Missouri. The chaplain at Ozarks Correctional Center, he has a sense of humor combined with a gift for telling stories that makes for compelling books and sermons. "The most important thing I've learned is showing radical love to others. Radical love is more important than knowing and teaching exactly the right things."

Day #204—Dad and I left for the *Field of Dreams* movie site. We connected with Joel Goldberg, the KC Royals pregame and postgame show announcer. "It's all about relationships."

Day #205—Nate Bukaty is the voice of *Sporting KC* on Sports Radio 810 WHB in KC. While Donald Trump was landing at Kansas City International Airport, Nate said, "Never burn any bridges. No matter how much you might feel slighted or wronged, never burn any bridges. When you've been treated unfairly, do the opposite. The positive comes back around. That's true for all of life, too."

Day #206—At the *Field of Dreams* with Dad, Bob Dyer, and Stan Sipka. No ghosts were seen, no voices heard. "I could live in Iowa," Dad said.

Day #207—On the way home from *Field of Dreams*, Dad and I connected with Moonlight Graham. Tim Flattery hosts *The Moonlight Graham Show* and is preparing to play a game on the *Field of Dreams* with his baseball family against a team of all-stars from England, Ireland, and Scotland—the Fort Dodge Gypsum Eaters against the Kent Buccaneers.

Day #208—The Queen City Crush are sponsored by Fellowship of Christian Athletes and play in the Show-Me Collegiate League, a forty-game wood-bat league at U.S. Baseball Park. Logan Rycraft is a middle infielder who volunteered to play catch after devotions before the game. "God can do great things through broken people."

Day #209—Aaron Unthank drove from Jacksonville, Florida, to Springfield, Missouri, on his way to Nashville, Tennessee, just to play catch with me.

Day #210—Brandon Smith moved to Springfield from Chicago to work in the travel industry. When he played baseball collegiately, he was the last person chosen for the travel team. He always had to wear the uniform of the previous day's starting pitcher, which meant his uniform number changed daily, as did the position he played.

Day #211—Evie Kennedy, a soon-to-be second grader, greeted me in Royals Blue Crew gear. She wants to be a gymnastics teacher and loves the movie *Moana*.

Day #212—Adam Stoddard is a pastor of Hope and Anchor Church and runs 100-mile races. "When I push myself to a place I've never been before, experiencing discomfort and suffering, I can learn something about myself I've never known before. We truly find out who we are only when pushed to extremes."

Day #213—Kristen Gammon was the president of my senior class at Kickapoo High School. We played catch on school property in memory of Mr. Nichols, our sophomore English teacher.

Day #214—Guy Newcomb is known throughout southwest Missouri and beyond for his Friday-night call-in radio show and website with scores posted from teams all over. The title of both his show and his Twitter handle are simple and brilliant: Scoreboard Guy.

Day #215—Sam Howard and I share a birthday month. Out in front of the Tower Theater where his dad is a deejay, Sam and I played catch while his sister Lilly added color commentary to his stories. She, too, got in on the catch playing.

Day #216—Hershel Wapp is a fifth-grader and a Royals fan, and played third base for the Regulators this summer. He likes to read the Goosebumps series and Harry Potter books and wants to be a journalist. His dad, "Almost Dr." Jaymes Wapp, is the principal of a school in Conway, Missouri. My favorite piece of wisdom that Almost Dr. Wapp passed along originated with *his* dad: "When you get hit below the belt, hold your elbow."

Day #217—At an open workout for the Grip 'N' Rip League, I convinced coach Justin Skinner to play catch in center field. Justin, a former Drury University player, coached his team to win the GRBL championship last year. He now works as a graphic artist at Prixel Creative. "Part of being creative is showing up every single day ready to work. Put in the time, do the hard work."

Day #218—Jay Miller and I were classmates at Kickapoo taking geometry and physics classes together and were soccer teammates our freshman year. Jay now teaches high school math and helps coach the track team. "Every deficiency you walk by, you're setting a new standard."

Day #219—Kody Cook works in the world of insurance and was willing to take a risk on a rainy-day catch. Neither one of us melted in the steady downpour. "Work hard and help others get what they need and you'll find that your needs will also be met."

Day #220—Kyle Moats is the athletic director at Missouri State University. "There is no substitute for hard work. That aspect of one's character—the willingness to do hard work—carries over to all aspects of life."

Day #221—Steve Pokin is a columnist for the *Springfield News-Leader*. He started writing in Springfield in March 2012 and is counting down to his one thousandth column. "I can make anything I write better by going over it again. I'm never at a point where I think it's perfect. Anything I write, I can improve."

Day #222—Don West, a freelance sports reporter and announcer, has called more than 3,600 games in the Springfield community and elsewhere. "Thirty-three years ago today, I did my first sports broadcast. When sports are your livelihood, everything you do is game prep. It just becomes part of who you are."

Day #223—Chicago Cubs fan Andy Robertson is the sports reporter at the *Log Cabin Democrat* and plays softball regularly even though he tore a muscle in his throwing arm. He has visited Wrigley Field with his wife, and shared stories of sports, faith, and life.

Day #224—Lindsey Overman and her daughter Skylar are living big, one bucket-list item at a time. Skylar, who has schizencephaly, has written a book raising awareness of the rare condition and advocating further research. "Love makes all dreams possible."

Day #225—Merry Yeager, a sports massage therapist specializing in neurokinetic therapy, gave me my first massage. Merry tests the strengths and weaknesses of paired muscles and then retrains the body through massage and follow-up exercises. "I really like helping people who are pushing themselves, who are seeing just how far they can go. I'm hoping some of that grit is contagious."

Day #226—Ryan Miller is a financial-advising former catcher who used to attend Missouri State's catching clinics. As a high school student, Ryan got the opportunity to be on the receiving end of major league pitches. "Cut fastballs would break feet. It was a pretty incredible experience catching pitchers who throw that hard."

Day #227—On the first day of their senior years in high school, as soon as school let out, Kaylea Bryan, Asa Scott, and Carson Marquart joined me for catch at the park. Carson is on cabinet this year and gearing toward the blood drive next week. Asa is in debate, where he and I met a couple of years ago when I was a judge. I encouraged them to make the most of the year.

Day #228—Crystal Quade is the Missouri state representative for district 132. Crystal ran for office to bring a perspective to Jefferson City that was lacking—millennial, female, and a thorough understanding of living in poverty. For a few seasons, Crystal was on the Springfield Roller Derby team. Her derby name was J. F. Slay, in honor of J. F. K. Her number was 1960. She now keeps a pair of rollerskates in her Jefferson City office.

Day #229—Holly Hesse has been the head coach of the Missouri State University softball team for thirty years. She pitched in three consecutive College World Series, has coached the Bears to five NCAA tournament appearances, and was inducted into the Missouri Sports Hall of Fame this past January. "There is no better training ground than sports for developing life skills and making a difference in the lives of student athletes. Teamwork, hard work, attitude, selflessness, mental toughness—I just love competition."

Day #230—With KC, Koby, Isaiah, and Grady at the Defenders Baseball skills clinic for a new homeschool team, where I briefly considered starting a coaching career. Simply walking from the van to the field, however, I strained my back and also briefly considered not playing catch. Thank God for IcyHot and ibuprofen.

Day #231— A before-church game of catch with Harper Satterfield and his sister Radley in which we got kicked off the neighboring property because they are starting a new business and don't have insurance yet for broken windows. We relocated to the church parking lot and didn't break any car windows.

Day #232—Kenyon Gerbrandt works for Literacy and Evangelism International in all things media related. His photo and video work has taken him around the world, interacting with new cultures and meeting amazing people and eating new foods. He said fried caterpillars taste like dirt, and I have no desire to confirm that.

Day #233—Judd Lasher turned his love of uniforms and logos into a simple hobby, creating sports memorabilia on mini football helmets, which is turning into a rapidly growing business—417 Helmets. "I recently did a Beatles helmet. The stripe down the middle was a few notes from 'Hey Jude.'"

Day #234—According to Coach Hesse (day #229), "Sara Jones was the heart and soul of the [MSU softball] team. She is a phenomenal young woman." Sara learned how to be that kind of teammate through tragedy. Her dad's car was hit by someone who was texting while driving. "Because of that accident," Sara said while we played catch, "my perspective changed. I'm thankful the outcome truly is a best-case scenario—everyone is alive, everyone is okay. In fact, not too long ago Dad and I played catch. But it helped me reflect on the true purpose of the word *game*. A game brings joy, creates relationships, and pushes you to be a better you. You are so much more than the number on your back or your stat line. You are a human first."

Day #235—In his thirteenth year with the Downtown Springfield Association, Rusty Worley tossed a ball with me on the historic square. He's traveled to twenty-seven MLB ballparks, lacking only Seattle, San Francisco, and Miami. "I try to live by the motto, 'Bloom where you're planted.' I look for ways to make a difference where I'm at today. If I'm taking care of things where I am today, tomorrow will take care of itself."

Day #236—The day after announcing the first collegiate football game of 2018 on ESPN3, Corey Riggs agreed to a game of catch. Corey produces, directs, and announces sporting events across southwest Missouri on

Mediacom, ESPN3, and the Missouri State Bears Radio Network. "There is always a story to tell. I love shining a light on the high school kids who have hit the weight room and put in the work, watching them grind on the field."

Day #237—Chris Bork is a middle-school physics teacher, volleyball coach, and photographer. A Cubs fan, he still rewatches highlights of the 2016 season; I know the feeling well from the previous year.

Day #238—Debra Lacy played softball in high school on a team called the Smooth Operators. On MLB's Players Weekend, in the heat and humidity of late August, playing together after praying together is truly a fantastic way to start the week, to be sent out into the community to make new friends and discover their stories, too.

Day #239—Jackie Rehwald is the causes reporter for the *Springfield News-Leader*. "As a reporter, I get to know people who are so far out from my traditional circles, and that has really been amazing. Whenever I pop into their lives, usually something wonderful or something terrible has just happened to them. I get to share their stories, to meet people when they are in the middle of doing something incredible."

Day #240—Jason Hynson is the executive director of Victory Mission, a faith-driven organization that provides emergency relief through outreach services and long-term empowerment through programming and social enterprise. "There are just so many people who think they're done. They are worn out and tired and don't feel they have a place anymore. But if someone can work with them for just a little bit, can walk alongside them and give them hope, they'll see just how much they are needed. Second chance. New life."

Day #241—For four years, Max has been a barista at Mudhouse Coffee to put into motion his dreams of being a professional animator. "Be a careless artist, but a ruthless editor."

Day #242—Zach Cole is a senior at Springfield Catholic High School committed to playing baseball at Ball State University in Indiana, a Division 1 school in the Mid-American Conference. "If your dreams aren't big enough that people laugh when they hear them, then you're not dreaming big enough. It's not how hard the dream will be to accomplish, it's how hard you work toward that dream."

Day #243—Tyler Jeske is Director of Baseball Operations for the Missouri State Bears baseball team. He helps coordinate equipment and video and analytics and travel all the while organizing a top-notch hitting clinic for baseball coaches. "We're just scratching the surface of everything we can learn from analytics."

Day #244—Joseph Oswalt is my brother-in-law and the best jump-scarer in the family. "*Baseball, Donuts, and Cheese Dip* could be the title of your next bestseller." I have to write a first bestseller first.

Day #245—Debra Lacy and her daughters, Marvalous and Verity, joined me for catch after worship. While holding her baby son, Lincoln, Debra caught the ball and glove-flipped it to Verity, who caught it and returned the throw to me. We played and celebrated that "God's mercy is wonderfully unfair," as we heard in the morning's sermon.

Day #246—Greg Hoskins is a firefighter and an EMT who transforms old, beat-up gloves into wallets, watchbands, purses, and dog toys. His grandfather was a master carpenter and passed along his wisdom and skills to Greg, who used to refurbish furniture. A Royals wallet from Hoskins Leather Craft now decorates my writing desk.

Day #247—Brent Gilstrap is a realtor and counselor who supports greatness and tries to make the world smaller, one new friend at a time. I was stranger #111 in his project to meet 365 strangers in a year. We played catch and I was able to join in his Taco Tuesday Crawl effort to eat tacos at every taco establishment in town. Catch was fantastic; tacos were meh.

Day #248—Ethan Forhetz is a journalist and news anchor who has experienced going viral multiple times. A fan of the Cardinals, he got to play and report on the fantasy camp experience, with Bob Forsch having a locker next to his. After catch, the battery in my van died. He drove home to get his jumper cables and made sure I was mobile before he left for work.

Day #249—Austin Kendrick is a testicular-cancer survivor and the coach for the Parkview High School basketball and baseball teams. "Men, check yourself regularly. You just might save your life."

Day #250—At the Negro Leagues Baseball Museum, after a walking tour with president Bob Kendrick, playing catch with All-American Girls Professional Baseball League players Mary Moore and Terry McKinley Uselmann on the appropriately named Field of Legends.

Day #251—Taiki is a twenty-year-old student at Kokushikan University studying sports biomechanics, training, and conditioning. A fan of Shohei Ohtani and Yu Darvish, he was in Springfield to perform judo at the Japanese Fall Festival put on by the Springfield Sister Cities Association.

Day #252—Chris Jarratt is Creative Director at Revel Advertising. "Swing for the fences. Some people will think it's awesome, and some won't. You've just got to give it your best effort. You've gotta have a quarterback mentality. Pick yourself up, dust yourself off, and keep going."

Day #253—Prolific sports announcer Tom Ladd met me at The FED, the baseball field of New Covenant Academy, and connected me with coach John Hartley and players Ryan Rogers and Ryan Carmack. The two seniors are committed to playing baseball collegiately and got a kick out of using the old Wilson.

Day #254—In 2002, Jason Hart spent ten days in the major leagues, accruing fifteen at bats for the Texas Rangers. In 2003, he played while a tumor grew in his brain. In 2004, Jason had surgery. Now the hitting coach for the Frisco RoughRiders, Jason played two more seasons in minor league ball to prove he could do it. "I think that if you respect the game, it will take care of you in the long run. Do the hard work and even if you don't get what you're shooting for, you can sleep well at night."

Day #255—The Arc of the Ozarks held a party at my church, a barbecue and car wash for Arc workers. Jamil, Christopher, Harvey, and Scott all played catch with me in the parking lot, carefully avoiding the newly washed vehicles. "Working at The Arc teaches patience," multiple people said. In our instant-everything culture of always faster, always now, patience is an often-forgotten virtue.

Day #256—Therapy catch with Aaron Unthank, who was in Springfield for his grandmother's funeral.

Day #257—Cody Pentecost is the GM of the Queen City Crush and is passionate about baseball and the Fellowship of Christian Athletes. "I played for the Niagara Power and walked away with my life transformed. That summer was the first opportunity I was challenged to really live out my faith."

Day #258—Shaun Lamie came to Springfield and received a catch-playing tour of the Queen City.

Day #259—Shane Lamie woke up early for the second day of the catch-playing tour before braving all the rollercoasters of Silver Dollar City. I wore a Cubs jersey to honor losing a bet we had made.

Day #260—Just before her taekwondo lessons, under a setting sun and blue skies, Sophie played catch wearing a taekwondo gee and told me of her passion for creating art to sell in preparation for a school trip she is taking to Costa Rica.

Day #261—When I lived in Lee's Summit, I watched Caleb play baseball for his high school. Former Drury University outstanding shortstop, Caleb Cole is the assistant general manager for the brand-new Redline Athletics Youth Training Center.

Day #262—Dr. Bill Powers is in his first year as the principal of Kickapoo High School. "Every day is a new day, and you have to have grace, especially with young adults. Because there will be days when they feel like they are going through the worst day of their lives, they need to be reminded that it will be okay. Treat everyone with grace."

Day #263—I was invited to Conway High School on the first day of the Baseball Fall Classic to spend a day sharing catch-playing stories with elementary and high school students. After class, I played catch with assistant principal Tyler Vestal, followed by several members of the baseball team. I caught a bullpen session, warming up the starter and eventual game-winning pitcher, and threw out my first (and only) first pitch.

Day #264—On the day President Trump visited Springfield, I played catch with Missouri State University president Clif Smart while security helicopters watched from above. Under Smart's leadership, MSU has set new enrollment records as well as increased retention and graduation rates. He gave great advice for parents of future college students: "Let them become independent. Give them some space to make decisions on their own. And let them trust their hearts and study something they really love."

Day #265—The morning of The Battle for Bell 3, Kameron Bell shared stories of her dad from a bullpen at the field at Glendale High School. "Dad was nice to everyone; it was just how he acted all the time. He stressed that we didn't know everything other people were going through and that being nice, being kind, is something we can always do. Making that extra effort to go out of your way and put a smile on someone's face can really make a big difference."

Day #266—Katrina High is an artist and comedienne and storyteller and librarian and owner of the rabbit Eleanor the Nibbler of Souls. I cannot wait to hear how she uses our game of catch as fodder for one of her routines.

Day #267—Ten-year-old Ethan Winget is a pitcher, middle infielder, and center fielder who loves the Harry Potter books and movies. He dreams of one day playing for the Royals, and I encouraged him to never, never give up.

Day #268—President of OneSource Insurance Group, Mark Acre is a former collegiate catcher and a St. Louis Cardinals fan who loves supporting and encouraging big dreams.

Day #269—Jeni Hopkins coached high school basketball for twenty-four years, accruing an impressive 332–206 record along the way. Her career coaching highlights include final four appearances, state runner-up and showmanship awards, and coaching some of the top talent in the country. We played catch in the radio studio parking lot before I appeared as a guest on her show, *A Coach's Perspective*.

Day #270—Played catch with Chandler Veit and his son Rylan, an eight-year-old who loves Cardinals players Yadier Molina and José Martinez. Chandler played baseball at Mansfield High School and told me stories of pitching against rival high schools and playing all nine positions his senior season.

Day #271—Ben Hammitt played baseball collegiately for Oklahoma Christian University and now plays in the local Grip 'N' Rip League on Sundays in the fall. A fan of Nolan Ryan—"I saw him pitch his last game"— Ben helps coach baseball during his free time. "There's just something about this game and the way it brings people together."

Day #272—At the Ballparks of America in Branson, Missouri, five different MLB fields from across the country are created in turfed replicate. Kyler Rose from Overland Park, Kansas, caught me fiddling with the old Wilson and asked, "Is that Shoeless Joe Jackson's glove?" He suggested this book be titled *A Baseball Year*.

Day #273—Matt McCoy patrolled center field for my Kickapoo High School baseball team. He's now a chaplain for Faith Hospice of the Ozarks, and we played catch on the last day of MLB's regular season. "I get the privilege to be reminded of what is most important each encounter I have with those who are dying. Over the course of the past several years, one of the things I'm learning is that regardless of whether I agree with you, we can still be friends."

Day #274—Kyndal Hawkins is a photographer on the go. She is slowly working on her new home so she can live in a van down by the river. Literally. A white cargo van transformed on the inside to be a home, complete with solar power and running water. "I love to travel and explore this big world we live in."

Day #275—Holly Fees was a paraprofessional in Jamie's classroom the second year Jamie taught and has become a dear family friend. She brought Dr Pepper and chocolate cake and her glove to dinner. "There's just something about baseball compared to other sports, but it's hard to describe. Like a feeling of home."

Day #276—Rick Theule took a road trip with his son to meet some internet friends in real life—a 2,560-mile road trip. "I forgot to pack my glove," he confessed upon arriving at Chez Bryan. A Detroit Tigers fan, Rick knows what it takes to start and finish something. "If I want to, if I put my mind to it, there's nothing I can't do. Which is cool, but also scary. The question is, 'Do I really want to do it?'"

Day #277—On a break from college while he decides which direction to go next, Noah Theule is learning to live with the daily courage and freedom to truly be himself. Keep searching the skies and dreaming big, Noah!

Day #278—Mark Goodwin attended Delaware Elementary School with me and was the goalie on the YMCA soccer team Dad coached. And then I learned that Aaron from Florida (day #170) is his cousin. What a small, small world.

Day #279—Missouri State's baseball team had their alumni game, and I figured if I packed a couple of gloves, I should be able to find someone willing to play catch with me. Tim Northern and Raj Suresh are stand-up comics who were in Springfield to perform and dropped by the game to pass some time. They gave me an education in comedy, cricket, and the courage to make new friends.

Day #280—Mike Hudgens is the photographer for the Grip 'N' Rip Baseball League, the men's wood-bat league at U.S. Baseball Park in Ozark, Missouri. "I'm just trying my best to capture everything, to make these guys look better than they really are. Really, all these guys are great guys. Their talent is secondary to who they are as people. They are what makes this league great."

Day #281—Jerry Elliott attended the 2018 Royals Alumni Fantasy Camp in Surprise, Arizona. At eighty-one years of age, Jerry played both infield and outfield and drove in his team's first run of the camp. He was awarded the trophy for Most Inspirational Player on Team Black.

Day #282—Creekside at Elfindale is an independent living retirement community. Bethany Burrows is Life Enrichment Coordinator at Creekside and asked if I'd be interested in sharing stories and playing catch. Ken, Martha, Mark, and Bethany all participated in the catch above the dining room.

Day #283, Part 1—Brian Rose, Kyler's dad (day #272), was in Springfield and wanted to see how it felt playing catch with an old glove. Brian was a second baseman who then played outfield and now helps coach both of his sons. Sharply dressed and coming straight from a presentation with Mercy Hospitals, Brian swung by my house before starting the return trip home.

Day #283, Part 2—Ryan Wolfe (day #100) and I played catch as we talked about getting the chance to play in the championship game of the Grip 'N' Rip League. We finalized plans to have a catch-playing World Series watch party at CY Sports Center.

Day #284—I had volunteered to help at Missouri State University's 38th Annual Children's Literature Festival. More than seventeen hundred students from twenty-four schools across southwest Missouri gathered to be inspired by and educated about the wonderful ways words are crafted into books. Author Antony John and MSU junior Shannon played catch with me at the break.

Day #285—Caleb and Kerry Davis are part of the weekday crew of the Bryan Family *Millennium Falcon*. After school and in the rain, a game of catch to welcome in the weekend.

Day #286—Justin Snider is the head coach of the Clever High School baseball team. He's coached one player in this year's College World Series finals and a pitcher who earned a September call-up with the Astros. "In a high school of 340 students, we've had twenty athletes go on to play college baseball in the last eight years."

Day #287—Tony Lewis is the founder and commissioner of the Grip 'N' Rip Baseball League. During the sixth inning of the championship game, after taking a swing off a tee as part of a gender reveal party (blue!), we played catch.

Day #288—Chloe Merced is the shortstop on the Kickapoo High School fastpitch softball team. She also is a forward on the basketball team and runs sprints and throws the shot put on the track team. She hit her first grand slam just a couple of weeks ago, securing a sizable Kickapoo victory, but didn't keep the ball. Her great-grandfather is Bill Virdon (day #61). "He just tells me to stay humble."

Day #289—Dr. Andrew Cline is a professor of media and journalism at Missouri State University and an award-winning documentary filmmaker with Carbon Trace Productions. He's working on a project capturing the mental health crises of the children in the middle of the Syrian war.

Day #290—Matt Bahun grew up in Omaha, Nebraska, going to the College World Series. When he played baseball in college, he once competed against Albert Pujols. "He hit a home run against us that was still rising when it cleared the fence. That ball was hit so hard it broke tree branches."

Day #291—Tom Hanks was wrong; there is crying in baseball. At the age of four, Cy went viral as the Saddest Little Cardinals Fan after a video was posted showing how upset he was at the Cardinals' lack of postseason success in 2012. Kris, Emily, Karen, and Bill Virdon joined in the game of catch following a baseball storytelling event.

Day #292—David Pennington is the fire chief of Springfield. "Collaboration is extremely powerful. Amazing things happen if you're willing to collaborate."

Day #293—For seven years, Derrick Docket was the social-media genius of the Missouri Valley Conference, covering every team in the valley. Ten collegiate teams. Eighteen sports. All by himself. "When you do a job you like, it's not really a job. It was a grind, of course, but I really liked it."

Day #294—For a hobby job, Lindy Snider works as an associate scout for the Los Angeles Dodgers. He started out scouting for the Colorado Rockies from 1994 through 2001 and has been with the Dodgers ever since. "The most important thing as a player is consistency. Are you consistently practicing properly, being a good teammate, throwing the ball right? The second most important thing is attitude. What is your daily attitude? Do you have the right mindset? In baseball, there are so many games, and every day you have to have the proper attitude." Bob Snider, Lindy's dad and a veteran of the Korean War, put on his Nokona glove that looked just like my old Wilson and tossed me the ball a few times—my first game of catch with a nonagenarian.

Day #295—Chandler is a senior at Ozark High School, plays second base for the team, and works at CY Sports. "This game is all about failure. You have to pick yourself up and keep going. If you dwell on it too long, you're setting yourself up for another mistake. Keep doing the hard work. Put in what you want to receive back."

Day #296—CY Sports hosted a World Series watch party. Seth Conner works in the Dodgers organization as the first base and hitting coach for the Great Lakes Loons, the Low-A team. He'll be heading to the World Series on Friday and predicted the Dodgers to win in seven.

Day #297—With Josh Kennedy's fifth- and sixth-grade classroom, the largest game of catch of the year: forty-two students.

Day #298—Patrick Queensen started Phelps Grove Outfitters to capture the creative spirit of Missouri one T-shirt at a time. He made Catch 365 T-shirts to support Springfield's Miracle League and to "Spread MO Love."

Day #299—Emily Weil is a Royals fan getting married to a Cardinals fan. On her wedding day, the same date that Don Denkinger made the infamous call of the 1985 World Series, we played catch and were joined by a dog named Egypt.

Day #300—For more than twenty-five years, Bob Reynolds was my parents' neighbor. He moved to a new neighborhood two years ago, and joined my family for a World Series watch party. My second game of catch with a nonagenarian.

Day #301—Carrie West, a Cardinals fan and my sister-in-law, had reconstructive shoulder surgery in high school and was the first person to employ a designated thrower, Christina Mossbarger. I threw the ball to Carrie, who caught it and flipped it to Christina, who threw it back to me. Christina's throwing arm was sore, however, because of the completion of a seven-hour tattoo session, finishing the sleeve on her right arm.

Day #302—At CY Sports, with David the junior pitcher from Glendale High School and Luke the "everything but catcher" sophomore from Kickapoo High School.

Day #303—Byron Hagler coached high school baseball for twenty-eight seasons, accruing all of baseball's best accolades, including back-to-back state championships. He's returning for his ninth season as the part-time assistant pitching coach at Drury University, where he coached Miami Marlins pitcher Trevor Richards for three seasons. "I would like to dedicate playing catch to Mom."

Day #304—Brock Phipps is the head groundskeeper at Hammons Field, home of the Double-A Springfield Cardinals. For the eighth consecutive year, Hammons Field was named the 2018 Texas League Field of the Year. Brock also won the Texas League Turf Manager of the Year. "I've learned a lot about patience. I have no control over Mother Nature."

Day #305—Clark "Moose" Nungester stopped in Springfield on his way to Arkansas from Kansas City. The rain stopped as soon as he hit the city limits. He encouraged me through stories of some of my favorite Royals players: Alex Gordon, Kevin Seitzer, and Buck O'Neil.

Day #306—Brian and Rachele Huett volunteer multiple times each week at Miracle League. For the last five years, Brian has pitched and Rachele has been his battery mate. They connected to the league through an article in the newspaper and love bringing joy and making new friends through the game.

Day #307—CY Sports Center hosted a collegiate baseball showcase. Keilynn, almost nine years old, was there to support his brother, Logan, a senior at Hollister who hopes to play next year. While aluminum bats pinged next to us, we played catch and strutted our abilities in front of the gathered collegiate coaches.

Day #308—Nya Jo Morgan hits home runs. For the last four years, she's been hitting homers at Ozark High School, setting a couple of school records in the process. Next year she'll be hitting homers at Southwest Baptist University. A catcher, Nya knows about leadership. "I know the importance of being a team player and not being bossy, but sometimes you have to say something."

Day #309—In 2008, Ryan Howerton was the Southwest Missouri Player of the Year. The former quarterback from the University of Missouri now coaches at Redline Athletics. "If you don't let other people help, you won't be as good as you could be."

Day #310—Coach Allen Gum is the head baseball coach at the University of Central Arkansas. While Kaylea toured the university, Coach Gum encouraged us with catch, free T-shirts, and an inspirational story about marbles.

Day #311—On the day we were scheduled to play catch, in the wee hours of the morning, there were multiple murders in Springfield. Since he is Springfield's chief of police, Chief Paul Williams notified me of his un-availability to meet as well as his desire to reschedule. We played catch today. "They're behind bars now," he said. New to the job, police spokeswoman Jasmine Bailey also joined in.

Day #312—Matt Vereen earned his journalism degree and moved to Springfield in July, where he is now the sports anchor at KOLR-10. "I like the stories of sports. Sports melts away a lot of the issues of the world and focuses in on one single moment. But the issues of the 'real world' are also played out through sports. In those moments, when you see the issues on the field, is where the journalism of sports journalism comes through."

Day #313—Bridgette Robles is a George Washington University grad-uate with a master's degree in strategic public relations. Bridgette also loves the stories that sports tell, interacting with fans on various social-media plat-forms, joining in as a bandwagon fan when necessary. She dreams of working in the communications department in professional baseball.

Day #314—Orioles fan Jim Doherty was chosen as one of the best EMTs in the Ozarks by *Springfield Business Journal*. On the day a new record low temperature was set, he told me of the adventures of the job. "Every day is different. That's what makes this job so much fun; no two days are the same. It's almost impossible to answer what I'll see over any given two weeks. Everything from 'Help! I've fallen and I can't get up' to heart attacks and strokes. I've even helped deliver three babies—the last one was breech."

Day #315—Matthew Bahun is seven and dreams of playing for the Royals, taking over Salvador Perez's position as catcher.

Day #316—Chris Brammer, the choir director from day #11, was the first person to notify me that I was an MLB.com notification. Today, in the middle of a steady November snowfall, he shared stories of the Alaskan cruise and vacation he and his wife took in July, which he had won. "The weather was absolutely perfect. We saw big brown bears much closer than you would want to see big brown bears."

Day #317—Dan Molloy is a Chicago White Sox fan and KOLR-10 sports anchor. Until he gets married, Dan is claiming October 26, 2005, as the best day of his life. On that day, the White Sox swept the Astros in the World Series, winning the championship for the first time in eighty-eight years. "I remember watching it with Dad, getting the big hug when it was over. It's just one of those memories that's burned into my brain."

Day #318—Rick Grayson is one of the best PGA teaching professionals in the country. He loves the Masters and the Royals and uses golf to spread joy throughout the community. Rick was inducted into the Missouri Sports Hall of Fame for outstanding contributions in the sport of golf and also was chosen as one of *Springfield Business Journal*'s 2018 Men of the Year. "I begin every day by thinking, 'Jack Nicklaus is coming in for a golf lesson.' I want to act and treat others in such a way as if they are Jack Nicklaus."

Day #319—Reverend Andy Bryan, of no relation that we could discover, is a seventh-generation Methodist pastor and Royals fan. "My first master's degree is in music, and I did that for five years. That's where I learned the most important thing—God's call is unique on each individual. Don't try to compare what God wants you to be doing to what someone else is doing. God's calling you to do something unique. I'm grateful for those years to discern that uniqueness of my call."

Day #320—Josh Payton, also catch partner on day #81, had surgery in August. Josh's stay turned from one night into four. His lung collapsed, his oxygenation levels dropped, and his pain was unmanageable. "I can't describe how scary it was to not be able to breathe and be in excruciating pain." I was thankful my friend was healthy again.

Day #321—Jimmy first learned how to do art in prison. He's now using his art to give hope to others, doing drawings during worship services at his church. "I pray over each piece and trust that God is going to lead me to give it to the right person. God is doing good things. I have hope for the future."

Day #322—As a junior at what was then called Southwest Missouri State University, Dick posted a 7–2 record with a 0.59 ERA—second best in the nation that year. Dick Jones is now the executive director of A Sporting Chance, which is celebrating its twenty-fifth anniversary. "ASC is here to be a positive force in the community, and we're doing it through sports."

Day #323—Chandler and Wyatt were working out at CY Sports Center a week after national signing day. Both are holding on to collegiate baseball aspirations. Baseball dreaming during football season.

Day #324—Doug Hatridge was the assistant superintendent for the Fort Osage School District when Albert Pujols moved to town. Doug's job was to make sure Albert could legally attend school. "Albert was a genuinely nice kid and humble. He never complained. He always said 'yes, sir' and 'no, sir.' I'm not sure he ever missed a day of school."

Day #325—Miracle Nic Fugitt has an amazing fastball. A Royals fan, an Alex Gordon fan, and an Elvis fan, Nick has Pelizaeus-Merzbacher disease—an extremely rare genetic disease that affects the myelin covering the nerves in the brain. There are less than fifteen hundred cases of PMD in the world. Nic is also full of contagious hope and talks of the day when he gets to heaven. "I'll walk and my first dance will be with Jennifer. I will play baseball and basketball and go fishing with my great-grandpa."

Day #326—On Thanksgiving Day, after brisket and cheesy corn and green beans and rolls and before Jamie's homemade apple pie, in my parents' back yard, I played catch with Dad and Kaylea and Sophie and Jamie.

Day #327—Jennifer, Chris, and Karsen Schumaker were in Springfield to celebrate Thanksgiving, run in the Turkey Trot, take a Hotel Vandivort selfie, and play catch. Jennifer crafts as The Little Wing to raise money for pediatric cancer research in honor of her nephew who died from acute myeloid leukemia two years ago.

Day #328—When he was in college, Topher Williams pitched until he couldn't throw the ball to home plate. He now plays on multiple travel softball teams because he can't get away from the game. "This game teaches respect for others."

Day #329—Springfield was under a wind advisory. Brothers Jaden and Asher Cooper and their cousins, Gabe and Landon Taylor, agreed to play catch in crazy curveball-inducing winds. After filling our bellies with hot dogs and chili, the four cousins and I walked to "the ditch" for catch and were joined by dad Gary Cooper and Sophie.

Day #330—Eric Lenz plays bass in the band at my church. Thanks to this catch-playing year, we learned that we are neighbors. We played catch while his across-the-street neighbor split firewood on his porch. "I keep my glove in my car, just in case my grandson wants to play catch."

Day #331—Ned Reynolds has been a sports broadcaster for sixty years. "Everyone I encountered on my broadcasting journey told me to be myself. And I've found those words to be true. Be yourself. Don't imitate others. And don't take yourself too seriously, either. You've gotta roll with the punches."

Day #332—Yankees fan and glove relacer Justin Perkins helped me track down gloves to donate as Christmas gifts to area kids. "I just can't pass up a chance to hook a kid up with a glove. Baseball is a big thing in my house."

Day #333—From 5:30 to 10 a.m., the morning show on 104.7 The Cave is hosted by Mike the Intern. Mike is an MSU grad and Chiefs fan with a degree in mass media production. He once won a contest taking a thousand selfies with a thousand different people in one month.

Day #334—Scott Bailes is a nine-year MLB veteran pitcher. In 1988, on opening day in Cleveland, Scott pitched a complete-game, three-hit shutout against the Baltimore Orioles facing the likes of Cal Ripken Jr., Eddie Murray, and Fred Lynn. "Baseball teaches you to be humble, above and beyond anything else. Don't ever believe people when they try and tell you how good you are. You're never as good as your good days. You're never as bad as your bad days. Just stay humble."

Day #335—Mark West is a musician and the owner of Downhome Productions. His CD, *Songs of the Game,* is the perfect soundtrack for Catch 365. The CD includes baseball songs by Tony Orlando, Kerry and

Tracy Cole (of The Lefty Brothers), Randle Chowning (founder of Ozark Mountain Daredevils), John Schlitt (of Petra), and Bob Walkenhorst (of The Rainmakers).

Day #336—For twenty years, The Finish Line was the locally owned sporting goods store in Springfield, and Dick Pogue was the owner. "We weren't making any money and I was working seventy hours a week, but I loved it. I miss the people."

Day #337—Dr. Joanna Cemore Brigden, an associate professor at MSU, understands the importance of play because she is a board member for both the America Association for the Child's Right to Play and The Association for the Study of Play. "Play is vital for healthy living, for enjoying life. People don't realize how important play is. It's vital for happiness. Everybody needs play in their life."

Day #338—Since 2005, Mark Harrell has been the photographer for the Double-A Springfield Cardinals. He also drove in the first two runs ever scored in the history of the Kickapoo High School baseball program. "To tell you the truth, what I've learned is that everyone is human. Celebrities, athletes, everyone. We're just fully human, and that's a good thing."

Day #339—Bethany Burrows organized my game of catch on day #282 at Creekside. The life enrichment coordinator knows how important stories and play are for all ages. "We tend to get caught up with our to-do lists. It is so important to take the time to completely relate to each person, living out, as much as possible, that whoever is in front of you at that moment is the most important person in your life."

Day #340—Clint Gerlek now works at iHeartRadio. The former college pitcher played baseball at San Diego State on Tony Gwynn Field while Tony Gwynn was the head coach. "Ideas breed ideas. Share your ideas when you have them and good things happen."

Day #341—Three years after undergoing Tommy John surgery, while pitching for MSU, Nick Petree was named the 2012 Louisville Slugger National Player of the Year—the best collegiate baseball player in the country. It's testament to his attitude and what baseball has taught him about life. "Baseball is a hard game. It's just like life. Not everything goes your way. But you learn how to deal with adversity in such a way as to take positives from it. In life, if you can learn to look for the positives when negative things happen, when it seems that nothing is going your way, you'll avoid that emotional rollercoaster."

Day #342—Brett Holmes was drafted by the Pittsburgh Pirates in the twentieth round. He played thirty-four games in the Class-A Short Season New York–Penn League for the Williamsport Crosscutters. That first year, his team won the championship. The grandson of Bill Virdon (day #61), Brett still loves the game. "Baseball teaches you to trust those around you. You don't have to do everything on your own. You have teammates who are there to pick you up."

Day #343—Morgan Goss is a freshman at Kickapoo High School, a southpaw first baseman and pitcher who dreams of hitting the field for the MSU Bears in a few years. His best day on the field came a couple of years ago. "I went 5–5 with three doubles and a pair of singles and got the walk-off hit. It was a pretty good game."

Day #344—Scott Nasby is in his seventh season as the head coach of the Drury University baseball team. He played in the College World Series in 2003 as a part of the MSU team and spent the summer of 2006 in Italy coaching the Godo Knights baseball team.

Day #345—Marty Willadsen is the executive vice president for the Missouri Sports Hall of Fame. He's the person responsible for planning and executing all HOF events, like the Sports Enthusiasts Baseball Luncheon back on day #144. "It's a new job every day. This job teaches you how important it is to be nice to people."

Day #346—Paul Evans is entering his thirty-first year as the pitching coach for Missouri State University. He has worked with thirteen pitchers on their way to the major leagues. "Like anything in life, baseball is ultimately about relationships."

Day #347—Haleigh Johnson knows all the players on the Cardinals team, and they know her, too. A southpaw shortstop, Haleigh has a near-perfect memory, peppering me with questions about favorite players from across the league.

Day #348—I was invited back to Conway High School to witness the Hamels Foundation ceremony of giving cleats as a Christmas gift to the baseball and softball teams. Coach Clay Bilyeu has been the head coach of the baseball team for thirteen years. A catcher, he graduated from Conway in 2000 and was part of the Class 2A District 11 Baseball Championship teams in 1997 and 2000. This past fall, Coach Bilyeu won his 400th game against Morrisonville on the other day I went to Conway High School to play catch (day #263).

Day #349—Bethany Bishop played both basketball and softball—catcher and third base, bless her knees. Yesterday, she celebrated her three-year anniversary at People Centric Consulting Group, where she works as an operations specialist. "I empower people to take ownership of the things they do and work in their strengths. Don't let fear stop you. You can't be afraid to ask questions or take a risk."

Day #350—Before church, I played catch with Adam Lawrence and listened to his adventures of driving all over the Midwest. After church, I played catch with Evie and Sophie. Evie talked about needing a new glove. Sophie demonstrated her own improved throwing skills from this year. After lunch, Kaylea and I swung by Kickapoo to play catch and process college decisions. The more she talked, the greater the distances her throws covered.

Day #351—Greg Fisher knows what it feels like to tear a rotator cuff. He declined having surgery and simply let it heal on its own. A Royals fan, he plays catch regularly with his nephews. "I don't try and throw as hard as I used to, but I can still throw."

Day #352—Brad Zweerink, a friend from elementary school days, is a freelance photographer who connected me to Rachel Johnson, the director of exhibits and programming for the Springfield Regional Arts Council. In preparation for a book-launch party, we played catch and talked of baseball in Boston.

Day #353—Justin Perkins (day #332) gave new life to the old George Brett glove. New padding and blue laces, and it is good to go for another year of playing catch.

Day #354—Brian McHaney was my catcher in high school. Brian has hypertrophic cardiomyopathy and collapsed during a game his junior year. He now works at Delaware Elementary School, encouraging students and teachers alike. "You always threw strikes. Never hurt my hand, but you always threw strikes."

Day #355—Chris Ballard hoped his sons would learn one lesson as they hiked fourteeners and camped in the mountains of Colorado. He now pastors at Story Church, a calling which radically affects all parts of his life. "You can do hard things. I didn't know then what I know now. I am capable of so much more. I just have to push through the hard times."

Day #356—Kirk Nungester had to have Tommy John surgery after his junior year in high school. He moved to the outfield and kept hitting, getting a game-winning double in his first collegiate at bat. "Every time you step on the field, you get to feel like a kid again."

Day #357—Howard Greenwood coached baseball in Nixa, Missouri, for twenty-two years. "You cannot underestimate the power of encouragement. Encouraging a kid takes them a lot farther along to reaching their potential." His son, Patrick, now coaches in Clayton, Missouri. "Even the bad days on the field are good ones, but it is kinda hard to forget those 22–2 losses," Patrick said.

Day #358—In the winter of 1997, Alan Mahaffey was selected by the Chicago Cubs in the Rule 5 draft. He spent spring training 1998 in the major league camp. He stayed with the team until the last day of spring training. "I had a lot of my best days on the field. From the time I was a kid, I wanted to be a professional baseball player. I was doing what I wanted to do, chasing that dream, and did everything I could to make it. I got the chance to pitch against some of the best in the game and have no regrets."

Day #359—On Christmas Day, I played catch with my brother-in-law, Cory West. Now a pastor and high school teacher in Pearland, Texas,

Cory has the heart of a coach. "I want to help them think through their games. They need to be fully present for every point. The relationships you develop with the students through the practices and games is the best part of the job."

Day #360—The Spangler family—Sam, Emily, Anya, Kai, and Eden—are friends from when my family and I lived in Lee's Summit. Catching up through stories of life and the passage of time while playing catch is a much better and more beautiful way to connect than social media.

Day #361—Phil Hockensmith was in the army for twenty-one years and retired in 1992 as a lieutenant colonel and an infantry officer as a Russian specialist before teaching high school history classes at Kickapoo. "Baseball is such a complicated sport, and I can appreciate that. I was trained as an officer to always be looking ahead to the next battle. Managers can't just be thinking about this at bat and this pitch, but also the innings to come. We live in a world where things are changing faster than anyone could imagine, and young people need to be adaptable and flexible."

Day #362—Brett Johnston is the founder of Compass Rose, a business that creates enriching musical experiences throughout Springfield. "Helping connect musicians to play in their spaces, curating events, has been great. Patience is the key."

Day #363—Erica Leak traveled the country in college studying architecture. Now in Austin, she is bringing light to the world through the city's affordable-housing program. "There are a lot of challenges that go along with a city that is vibrant and changing. I'm helping manage that change and trying to make it a better place, a more equitable city."

Day #364—In March 2017, Billy Conway officially started Squints Apparel, making T-shirts inspired by life in Kansas City and the epic baseball movie *The Sandlot*. When the Buck O'Neil Education and Research Center was vandalized, Billy designed a special T-shirt and donated all proceeds from the sales to the restoration process.

Day #365—The Last Day of the 2018 Catch-Playing Tour of Kansas City: Dave Darby, Chris Browne, Darwin Pennye, Jeff Passan, Brandon

Nichols, Jesse McDaniel, Leslie Guyton, Alexis Guyton, Sabrina Guyton, Jake Mueller, Gabe Mueller, Brenna Mueller, Gracie Mueller, Katrina High, Kaylea Bryan, Sophie Bryan, and Nash High.

The end.